100 events that made history

Memorable moments that shaped the modern world

Penguin Random House

DK London

Senior project editor Steven Carton
Senior art editor Jacqui Swan
Editor Ann Baggaley
Jackets coordinator Claire Gell
Jacket design development manager
Sophia MTT
Producer, pre-production
Jacqueline Street
Producer Mary Slater
Managing editor Paula Regan
Managing art editor Owen Peyton Jones

Publisher Andrew Macintyre
Associate publishing director
Liz Wheeler
Art director Karen Self
Design director Stuart Jackman
Publishing director Jonathan Metcalf

DK Delhi

Senior editor Sreshtha Bhattacharya
Senior art editor Anjana Nair
Project art editor Vikas Chauhan
Art editor Heena Sharma
Assistant editor Charvi Arora
Assistant art editors Nidhi Rastogi,
Kshitiz Dobhal
Senior DTP designers Harish Aggarwal,
Neeraj Bhatia
DTP designers Pawan Kumar,
Mohammad Rizwan, Syed Md Farhan
Senior picture researcher Sumedha Chopra
Jacket designer Suhita Dharamjit
Managing jackets editor Saloni Singh
Managing editor Kingshuk Ghoshal
Managing art editor Govind Mittal
Pre-production manager Balwant Singh
Production manager Pankaj Sharma

First published in Great Britain in 2016
by Dorling Kindersley Limited
80 Strand, London WC2R 0RL

Copyright © 2016 Dorling Kindersley Limited

A Penguin Random House Company
2 4 6 8 10 9 7 5 3 1
001 – 264883 – February/2016

A CIP catalogue record for this book is available from the British Library.

ISBN 978-0-2412-2789-3

Printed and bound in Hong Kong

A WORLD OF IDEAS:
SEE ALL THERE IS TO KNOW

Discover more at
www.dk.com

100

events

that made

history

Memorable moments
that shaped
the modern world

Written by Clare Hibbert, Andrea Mills,
Rona Skene, and Sarah Tomley

Consultant Philip Parker

Contents

Social

firsts

It takes only a spark of genius or a bit of passion to make big things happen. Throughout history, the actions of a single individual or a collective group have revolutionized society, transforming the way people live. Influential ideas, powerful beliefs, grand ambitions, and brand-new breakthroughs have enriched entire nations and influenced future generations.

The first farmers

Hunter-gatherers dig their way to CIVILIZATION

By about 10,000 BCE, the wandering peoples of the prehistoric world had worked out that if you plant seeds, they grow. They gave up roving and hunting and began settling down to become farmers.

By the way...
We ancient folk didn't all toil on the land. Some of us had time for the arty stuff, like inventing pottery.

On the move

TRIBES of hunter-gatherers once **drifted from place to place**, looking for animals to hunt and plants to gather. People never had the chance to build a settled community because *they had to keep moving* in search of food and water.

What came after...

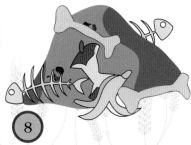

A community might give security, but for the first time people faced **SOCIAL ISSUES** such as rubbish disposal, overcrowding, and fast-spreading diseases.

By 8000 BCE, farming had sprung up in east Asia and the Americas. **MAIZE**, squashes, millet, and rice were top of the menu in these regions.

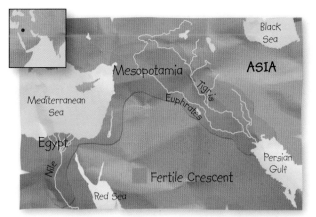

Cultivating the Crescent

Farming truly got going in an area known as the **FERTILE CRESCENT**. The region included Egypt and western Asia, and stretched from the Mediterranean to the Persian Gulf. When **three big rivers** – the Nile, Tigris, and Euphrates – flooded, their silt-loaded water *enriched the soil*, making it ideal farming land.

How it changed the world

A more reliable food supply often meant a surplus, which allowed people to do other jobs. This helped kick-start the first civilizations and some of the early farming villages went on to become big towns and cities.

Taming the beasts

Once people started farming, the **domestication of animals** followed rapidly. Dogs, goats, sheep, and pigs were among the first to be tamed by humans. Wild herds became a **CONTROLLABLE SUPPLY** of *meat, milk, and wool*.

Staying put

As fresh food could be grown to order and **AGRICULTURE** became the norm, the first real human societies formed. Where people **sowed crops** in fixed locations year after year, the farms became *natural centres of civilization*.

Did you know?

Remains of ancient people show that eating a lot of grain wore down their teeth, as grit from the soil got into their food!

Modern food crops, such as WHEAT, BARLEY, AND RYE, *replaced the original wild grasses of prehistoric times about 7000* BCE *in the Middle East.*

With crops being farmed around the world, the IMPORT AND EXPORT OF FOOD *became big business. This Roman grocer would have bought stock from many places.*

Handy to have

Things really started rocking about 2.5 million years ago (MYA), when an ancestral species to humans, the Australopithecines, became the first to hand-craft tools. They were followed by *Homo habilis* ("Handy man") who used rocks to sharpen **CUTTING EDGES**. These tools seem to have been used to scrape meat off animal bones, but **not for hunting or defence**.

Hand axes were often made from flint.

First tools

TRANSFORMING the lives of early humans

Given the chop

The leaf-shaped **handaxe** became the tool of choice for *Homo erectus* ("Upright man") for more than a million years. First created about 1.75 MYA, this revolutionary design had evolved from previous crude tools. The handaxe could be used for digging, hunting, chopping wood, or **MAKING OTHER TOOLS**.

Fire-starter

Though its **exact origins** are hotly contested, the control of fire lit up the lives of *Homo erectus*, providing warmth, light at night, and protection against animals. It also meant that early humans could really get **COOKING** – which scientists believe improved diet and led to a larger brain.

How it changed...

Rocks, handaxes, and fire all became crucial tools in helping early humans master their world.

the world

Homo erectus brains were roughly two-thirds the size of ours.

Using rocks or wood to create a spark was the easiest way to start a fire.

The Lascaux cave paintings depict many horses, stags, and bulls, plus a bear, a rhinoceros, and a human.

Painting the past

The world's oldest art is believed to be **cave drawings** found in **SULAWESI, INDONESIA**. About 40,000 years old, these drawings feature hand prints and hunting animals. It's possible that *art may have originated in Africa* before the creators moved to Asia to continue their craft.

Cave creatures

In 1940, a bunch of French teenagers found **paintings of animals** in the caves of Lascaux, France. These *amazing images date back 17,000 years*. The reason for their depiction remains uncertain, though it is possible that they were drawn to encourage **SUCCESSFUL HUNTING**.

Mane attraction

The oldest example of figurative art is the **Lion Man of Hohlenstein Stadel** (right). This statue, carved out of **MAMMOTH TUSK**, was created about 40,000 years ago in what is now modern-day Germany. It shows a human body with the head of a *European cave lion*.

How it changed... the world

Art probably served the same purpose for early humans as it does for us today – it educates, entertains, and decorates our lives.

First art

Decorating the HOMES and lives of early humans

Ur founded

The first CITIES provided the blueprint for other urban settlements to develop

The ziggurat may have been 30 m (98 ft) in height.

Top temple

Ur was **ESTABLISHED** on the riverbanks of ancient Mesopotamia (modern-day Iraq) about 3200 BCE. The city reached its peak under King Ur-Nammu, who went on a one-man mission to make **Ur the supreme city of Mesopotamia**. In the heart of the city was a ziggurat temple for the Moon god Nanna, who was the *patron god of the city*.

How it changed... the world

It's hard to imagine our world today without cities. Ur was the first to be worthy of the name.

The ziggurat was completed by Ur-Nammu's son Shulgi.

Set in stone

Ur-Nammu put the *city's builders to work*, as he strove to make Ur a centre of ground-breaking **ARCHITECTURAL ACHIEVEMENT**. Gradually, the barren landscape changed, with mud-brick buildings giving way to religious shrines, and decorative mosaics, made out of stone. The **world's first urban landscape** was created.

Territorial tension

As multiple city-states were established all over Mesopotamia, **WARS** broke out over who was on top. *The Standard of Ur* (left) depicts one such battle. **Armies fought** bloody battles, with many dying to control the land. Ur was abandoned about 450 BCE.

The Standard may have been mounted on a pole and carried into battle.

The Great Bath of Mohenjo-daro in Sindh, Pakistan, was probably used to purify bathers during religious rituals.

Cleaner cities

The **Indus Valley** civilization of modern-day Pakistan and northwest India was the first to get *serious about sewage*. They constructed public baths, but many homes also enjoyed a water supply, well, and a bath. They even had the first flushing toilets (but **TOILET PAPER** was about 3,000 years away in the future!).

Pipe dream

The world's first sewage system was up and FLUSHING in 2500 BCE

Indus Valley drain

Down the pan

All of this was possible because the Indus people constructed *advanced networks* of brick-lined underground **sewage drains** that took the waste and brought it to a river or cesspool. Separate pipes brought clean, **FRESH WATER** into cities.

How it changed...
As cities expanded, getting rid of waste became a big deal. Without a proper water system, illness and disease can spread quickly.
the world

Roman relief

The Romans were rather adept when it came to toilet matters too. They constructed **COMMUNAL TOILETS**, such as this example in Leptis Magna (in modern-day Libya). Up to 30 people would use the toilets together, *without any partitions between them*. A sponge on a stick did the job of toilet paper, and bathhouse water would **flush the waste** into sewers.

First powerful woman

The first great woman recognized in history is Hatshepsut, Egypt's most celebrated female pharaoh. She led the nation for more than 20 years, at a time when men usually ruled the roost.

Regent ruler

In 1479 BCE, Pharaoh Thutmose II **PASSED AWAY**, but his son Thutmose III was only a baby. His stepmother **Hatshepsut became regent**, leading on behalf of Thutmose III until he was *old enough to take control*.

Did you know?
Though Thutmose III was never deposed, it is clear that Hatshepsut was the real ruler.

What came before...

Upper Egypt crown   Lower Egypt crown   United Egypt crown

THE FIRST KING of Egypt was a man named Narmer in about 3100 BCE. He is thought to have joined the two parts of Upper and Lower Egypt into one.

Egyptian pharaohs invented the world's first state in 3000 BCE and were the first rulers to have elaborate burial customs such as DEATH MASKS (left).

Bearded lady

Hatshepsut *wasted no time* making her mark by establishing trade links and constructing major monuments. But this was still ultimately a man's world, so Hatshepsut dressed in the **full regalia of a male monarch**, including a kilt, crown, and an artificial beard. Artists always depicted her with a beard, and she was sometimes called **"HE"** in the documents of the time.

Curse of Cleopatra

Hatshepsut's achievements have been **OVERSHADOWED** by Cleopatra VII, whose turbulent reign from 51–30 BCE **brought an end to Egypt's pharaohs**. First ruling with her brothers, she later overthrew them to take sole charge. Losing to the Romans in the Battle of Actium proved too much, as she tragically *took her own life* with a snake's bite.

The snake was an Egyptian cobra.

By the way...
I married my brother Ptolemy XIII, and jointly ruled with him for a while. I then convinced Julius Caesar to get rid of him, and I ruled alone!

Tomb treasures

Hatshepsut, like all royal rulers, was buried in an **ornate tomb** inside a specially crafted temple. Kings and queens were laid to rest together with the **TREASURED POSSESSIONS** and everyday goods they had valued the most, to get them prepared for the afterlife. Cleopatra's tomb has *never been found*.

Hatshepsut was buried in a temple near the Valley of the Kings, Egypt.

How it changed the world

Though she had to appear and act like a male ruler to be taken seriously, Hatshepsut's great reign proved women could be just as good as – if not better than – men on the political stage.

*Pharaoh Djoser, who ruled from 2670 to 2651 BCE, constructed the **FIRST PYRAMID**, which was the first great stone building.*

AHMOSE-NEFERTARI *was among the first female rulers of Egypt in 1525–1504 BCE, acting as co-regent for her son Amenhotep I.*

Laws are written down

History's best-known legal document sets the law in STONE

By the way... My Code is written in cuneiform, an ancient script that some clever modern folk have learned to read.

The world's first truly civilized states arose in Mesopotamia (modern-day Iraq). This area is known as "the Cradle of Civilization" because it was where many ideas developed, including the wheel, writing, and an important code of law.

United rule

The heart of **Mesopotamia** was the city-state of Babylon. In 1760 BCE, after a series of wars, the powerful King **HAMMURABI** of Babylon crushed rival city-states to bring the whole of Mesopotamia under his rule. He didn't stop at being a conqueror. He *wanted his kingdom to evolve* and develop, so he masterminded building projects that created temples, canals, and aqueducts.

What came before...

From around 4000 BCE, the **SUMERIANS** prospered in the fertile lands around Mesopotamia's rivers. They formed city-states, each ruled by a king and government.

The **AKKADIANS** rose to power in the Middle East in 2300 BCE, creating the first united empire under one ruler.

Crime and punishment

King Hammurabi ruled Mesopotamia with an *iron fist*. He laid down the law and introduced severe punishments for bad behaviour. His set of laws became known as the "**CODE OF HAMMURABI**", and remains one of the earliest written records of laws. Etched in stone, the laws of the land were listed under a depiction of Hammurabi receiving the code from **Shamash**, the Babylonian Sun god of justice.

The King's eagerness to please the gods is shown on the stele.

Set in stone

STONE PILLARS bearing the Code of Hammurabi were displayed around his kingdom for all to see. Only one has ever been found, but it includes 282 laws grouped by subject, such as household, trade, religion, and slavery. **Most people couldn't read the script**, but law-breakers could expect to have their gnashers knocked out, or *end up skewered on spikes*. Ouch!

Scribes copied the script onto clay tablets for centuries afterwards.

Despite the strict laws, there was time for fun and games in Mesopotamia. The first ever board games were played here, and included ornate boards and set pieces.

How it changed the world

Although Hammurabi's Code seems too brash and brutal now, it paved the way for ground-breaking ideas at the heart of modern law. Most notably, the idea that a particular crime attracted a particular penalty, and that punishments should not be arbitrary. Both remain integral to many of today's legal systems.

What came after...

*The warlike **ASSYRIANS** took over in about 1200 BCE, destroying Babylon. Their clay tablets tell us much of what we know about Mesopotamian history.*

*The Persians under **CYRUS THE GREAT** established themselves in the Middle East from 550 BCE and conquered most of the Middle East.*

World religions founded

Different ways of explaining life and the UNIVERSE

Shiva, one of the most powerful Hindu gods, is sometimes shown as a dancer.

The major world religions are very old. Each in its own way has shaped the lives of millions of people over thousands of years. These religions have also had a huge effect on other parts of life like art, buildings, learning, and music.

Hinduism

Unlike many religions, Hinduism was *not founded by one person* and does not have one set of rules. Its beliefs **date back 4,000 years** to the Aryan people of northwest India. **BRAHMA**, the creator, is the chief god among the many whom Hindus worship. Their sacred writings include verses called the Vedas. There are 900 million Hindus worldwide.

Did you know?
Both Buddhists and Hindus believe in a cycle of birth, death, and rebirth in a new body (reincarnation).

Buddhism

An Indian prince named **Siddhartha Gautama,** born in 563 BCE, rejected his riches when he saw what suffering there was in the world. After years of fasting and hardship, he sat beneath a tree to do some *serious thinking*. He learned that happiness comes from getting rid of bad feelings. He is known as **THE BUDDHA** ("awakened one"). Today, 488 million people follow his teachings.

Judaism

Arising in the **Middle East** more than 3,500 years ago, Judaism is the religion of the **JEWISH PEOPLE**. It was the first major faith to believe in one God. The history of Judaism and the laws by which believers should live are found in the *Hebrew Bible*, or Old Testament. The religion has about 14 million followers.

A seven-branched sacred lamp called the menorah is used in Jewish religious ceremonies.

The Bible says that Jesus performed more than 30 miracles.

Christianity

Christianity is the **largest world religion**, with two billion followers. Christians believe that a man named *Jesus Christ*, born in the Holy Land in about 4 BCE, was the Son of God. The religion is based on **THE BIBLE** – which combines the Old Testament with Christ's teachings (known as the New Testament). The Romans were convinced that Jesus was a dangerous influence and killed him, but Christians believe his spirit is still alive.

The black granite Kaaba in Mecca, Saudi Arabia, is a sacred Muslim site, visited by millions of pilgrims every year.

Islam

The founder of Islam was born in Mecca (modern-day Saudi Arabia) in 570 CE. Named Muhammad, he was a prophet who taught his followers to worship **ONE GOD, ALLAH**. Islam is the second-largest world religion, with a billion or more believers called **Muslims**. They follow holy laws written in scriptures called the *Qur'an*, pray five times a day, and fast during the month of Ramadan.

The teachings of Confucius

Ideas for making rulers more JUST

The 6th-century-BCE Chinese philosopher known as Confucius spread the idea that societies should be run fairly. His rules for making this happen still influence people today.

Tough start

Confucius was born in 551 BCE near the city of Qufu in China. After his father died, the family were **VERY POOR** and the young Confucius had to do jobs to *support his family*. He still managed to keep up his studies and sit difficult exams to qualify as a **civil servant**.

On the road

Working as a *government official*, Confucius was shocked by the unfairness of China's rulers. He became a minister, but gave up his career to **GO TRAVELLING**. This was no gap year. For 12 years he roamed round China, spreading his **ideas on social equality**. Once back home, he spent the rest of his life teaching.

What came before...

The earliest known Chinese writing found is on **ORACLE BONES** *from the Shang Dynasty (c.1600 BCE–1046 BCE). Experts thought the Shang were a myth, but the writing showed otherwise.*

*China's first true philosopher was **LAO TZU**, who lived around 600 BCE. He founded a religion called Taoism, which is based on honesty and harmony.*

Happy ever after

Confucius had a simple recipe for a happy life: people should **be nice to each other**, with the ruler setting an example. He made **five rules**, which he called the **FIVE VIRTUES**. These were *Yi, Li, Ren, Zhi,* and *Xin* – with each one crucial for a happy and worthwhile life.

義 *Yi* is the virtue of honesty and integrity.

禮 *Li* is the virtue of correct behaviour and propriety.

仁 *Ren* is the virtue of charity and humanity.

智 *Zhi* is the virtue of Knowledge and learning.

信 *Xin* is the virtue of faithfulness and loyalty.

By the way… Confucius probably didn't write any books himself. His sayings were collected and written down by his followers.

Getting the message

It was only **after his death** that Confucius's message really got through to people. In 136 BCE, the philosopher's ideas were officially adopted in China as a central part of the country's policy. *Confucianism,* as the system came to be known, lasted for the **NEXT 2,000 YEARS**.

How it changed the world

In Confucius's time, it was a pretty startling idea that rulers should behave well and treat their subjects kindly. The philosopher's suggestions helped to pave the way to fairer societies.

What came after…

Chinese philosopher **MENCIUS** *(372–289 BCE)* took Confucius's ideas a stage further. He instructed people to join together to overthrow unjust rulers.

The third president of the United States of America, **THOMAS JEFFERSON** *(1743– 1826), was influenced by the philosophies of Confucius.*

One-day event

Olympia, a **religious centre** in southwest Greece, played host to the first Games in 776 BCE, thrown to honour Zeus, the protector and ruler of humans. The **ONE-DAY EVENT** got off to a running start with just one competitive sport – the *men's 200-m (650-ft) sprint*.

The statue of Zeus at Olympia was one of the seven wonders of the ancient world.

How it changed...

The Olympic Games started the tradition of different nations coming together to compete peacefully against each other.

the world

First Olympic Games

Nearly 3,000 years ago, a SPORTS event dedicated to the Greek god Zeus was held

This coin shows the head of spoilsport Emperor Theodosius.

Bigger and better

As the Games evolved over time, more competitions were included and the event was extended to **FIVE DAYS**. Boxing and chariot-racing got under way, while the **pentathlon** featured discus, javelin, running, wrestling, and long jump. *Wreaths of olive leaves* were awarded to the winners, who went home as heroes.

A wrestler won if he threw his opponent to the ground three times.

Dangerous times

Internal wars made Greece a dangerous place. When the Olympic Games were on, a **ceasefire** was announced so that athletes and spectators could pass through enemy lines. The Games kept going, with events being held *every four years* until 393 CE, when Christian Emperor Theodosius **BANNED** the fun as immoral.

22

Political vision

In city-states of ancient Greece, government was once entirely in the hands of the *richest section of the population*. A few wealthy **aristocrats** controlled property, parliament, and finances, and no one else had a say. In 507 BCE, an Athenian statesman called Cleisthenes reformed this **UNFAIR SYSTEM** by giving ordinary citizens political rights.

Athenian democrats held political meetings at a place called the Pynx.

Cleisthenes is known as the "Father of Athenian democracy".

Not fair enough

Cleisthenes' system, the first democracy, consisted of three bodies: the **ekklesia** wrote laws and policies; the **BOULE** was a citizens' council; and the *dikasteria* were the civil law courts. But the system wasn't that fair. Out of a population of 300,000 people, only 30,000 or so free men had the right to vote. Women, slaves, and foreigners didn't count in this democracy.

Dawn of democracy

How the rule of the PEOPLE first came about

Sign of the times

The new democracy *lasted for two centuries* and was a powerful era for Athens. In this period, the city's most famous landmark was created – the **PARTHENON**, a temple dedicated to the goddess Athena. It was a sign of change that the temple was decorated with illustrations of **ordinary people** for the first time in history.

How it changed...

Ancient Athenian democracy wasn't perfect, but its ideal of political rights for all is the blueprint for many states today.

the world

Black Death

A mystery PLAGUE causes panic

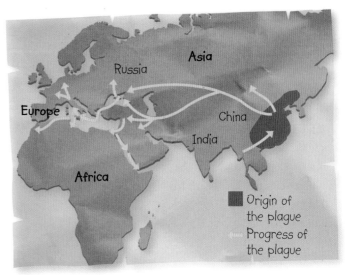

In the 14th century, a terrible disease wiped out a third of the population of Europe, as well as millions more in Asia and Africa.

Crisis in China

A highly contagious **INFECTION**, known as the plague or the Black Death, arose deep in Asia. The disease gripped central China in 1333, and **spread fast**. As a centre of trade, China was visited by merchants from countries all over the world – *who took the plague home with them*.

The disease was most likely caused by bacteria passed on in bites from fleas carried by rats.

Plague in Europe

The Black Death reached Europe in 1347 and lasted until about 1353. The **plague's jumping-off point** from Asia was probably the Crimea. Here, Mongol warriors, laying siege to the city of Kaffa, *catapulted their infected corpses* over its walls to weaken the defenders. This port was colonized by the Genoese, whose **TRADING SHIPS** carried the disease to Sicily.

Big swellings, called buboes, were among the horrible symptoms.

What came before...

In about 250 CE, the **ROMAN EMPIRE** *was hit by the Plague of Cyprian. At its height, the disease, which was probably smallpox, killed about 5,000 Romans a day.*

There was an even worse outbreak in Constantinople (modern-day Istanbul) in 541 CE. The **PLAGUE OF JUSTINIAN** *wiped out 10,000 people a day.*

No cure

Medieval medicine wasn't cutting edge. *Bacteria* had not yet been discovered. People thought diseases were caused by "bad air". The only treatments doctors could offer – such as herbal brews and blood-letting – had **ZERO EFFECT** on the relentless plague. People said **God had sent the Black Death** to punish them for their sinfulness. They prayed for forgiveness, but still the horror went on.

Plague doctors wore masks with beaks stuffed with herbs that were meant to give protection from the plague.

How it changed the world

The Black Death tore the social structures of Europe and Asia apart, destroying whole families and decimating cities.

Did you know?
A few cases of plague still occur every year. Today, the disease can be cured quickly with antibiotics.

Victims had a high fever and coughed up blood. Their skin was blotched purple.

What came after...

When a huge fire destroyed much of **LONDON IN 1666**, it wasn't all bad. The flames put an end to the recent plague that had killed 100,000 English people.

In 1918, **A STRAIN OF INFLUENZA**, known as Spanish flu, is thought to have killed up to 50 million people – 3 per cent of the world's population.

Hidden riches

In 1545, the world's **greatest source** of silver was found hidden inside a mountain, the high-altitude **CERRO POTOSÍ** (in present-day Bolivia). Within a year of the discovery, the Spanish conquerors of South America had built a *mining town* there, triggering a silver rush.

Striking silver

The 16th-century discovery of SILVER in Potosí gave Spain unimaginable wealth

How it changed...

The riches at Potosí helped to make the Americas a "go to" destination. More people poured in and built colonies.

the world

Deadly mines

The new mines made the Spanish *top traders* in the Americas for two centuries. They shipped out more than **40,000 TONNES** of silver from Potosí. Local people, joined by imported African slaves, were **forced to work in the mines** in terrible conditions. Many died from accidents, illnesses, and brutal treatment.

Coin made of silver mined at Potosí.

Silver city

By the 17th century, the scruffy camp at Potosí had become a **wealthy city**. The silver helped to pay for Spain's wars in Europe. A huge percentage of the silver ended up in **CHINA**, where it was used for currency and *traded for tea, silk, and porcelain*.

Potosí is still mined today, but most of the silver is gone.

About 100 Puritans sailed with the Mayflower.

American dream

A group of English men and women known as **Puritans** decided they'd had enough of being hated for their religious beliefs. They wanted to reform the Protestant Church of England, which didn't win them many friends. Following their **DREAM** of a new life, they left for America in a ship called the *Mayflower* in 1620.

Pilgrims set sail

Religious persecution in 17th-century Europe drove the PURITANS to America

Rough voyage

Loaded with supplies and livestock, the *Mayflower* sailed from Plymouth **across the Atlantic Ocean**. It was a long and stormy voyage. The seasick travellers we now know as the **Pilgrim Fathers** finally landed on the **MASSACHUSETTS**, USA, coast, and named the area Plymouth.

First Thanksgiving

Many Puritans **DIED** on the voyage and in the first icy winter in America. Glad to be alive, the survivors held a big feast in 1621, the original *Thanksgiving*. Local Native Americans joined the party. They showed the newcomers how to work the land, and the Pilgrims built up a **successful colony**.

How it changed... The Pilgrims paved the way for more colonists and the growth of trade. They are regarded as the founders of the United States of America. **the world**

27

Agricultural revolution

A crop of new ideas leads to a BOOM in food production

Townshend came to be nicknamed "Turnip Townshend".

Tull's seed drill cut furrows in the soil before sowing.

Seed spreader

Farmers used to scatter seed on their fields **by hand**, which was slow and wasteful. In 1701, Englishman **JETHRO TULL** invented a *seed drill machine*. Drawn by a horse, this contraption dropped the seeds in neat rows.

Cream of the crop

In the 1700s, England tried a **new crop system**, devised by politician Charles Townshend. Wheat, barley, turnips, and clover were grown in a different field every year in a four-year cycle. The **ROTATION** meant healthy soil and *big harvests*. Cattle were grazed in some fields to add extra fertilizer!

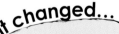
How it changed...

The Agricultural Revolution increased the efficiency of farming, and led to larger hauls of crops and meat.

the world

Pastures new

The new ideas in farming meant that less people were needed to work the land. In England, a **NEW LAW** let landowners *fence off land* for their private farms. With farm land being snapped up, and fewer people needed in the countryside, many **moved to the cities** to make a living.

The beefy Dishley Longhorn cattle were specially bred to provide more meat for a growing population.

28

Industrial Revolution

Machines rule and workers move from fields to FACTORIES

Coal mining became crucial to the success of the Industrial Revolution.

Stephenson started his career in coal mines looking after the steam machinery used there.

Steam up

In the 19th century, vast **textile factories and mills** with newly invented steam-powered machinery sprang up all over England. **COAL** production soared to fuel these *growing industries*.

On the right track

Steam engines had been running on public railways for four years when English engineer George Stephenson launched his locomotive *Rocket* in 1829. This champion chuffer won the speed race on the **NEW RAILWAY** from Liverpool to Manchester, zipping along at 47 kph (29 mph).

Young children like these cloth-mill workers often did hard, dangerous jobs.

Grim life

As **industry replaced agriculture**, country folk turned into city dwellers. Masses of people filled towns and cities looking for **WORK**. Conditions were grim, with crowded houses, long shifts for terrible pay, and dangerous jobs. *Even children worked*, with workplace accidents and poor health common.

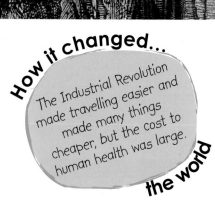

How it changed...

The Industrial Revolution made travelling easier and made many things cheaper, but the cost to human health was large.

the world

Slaves were shackled for the long journey.

Slave trade

Spanish traders sent the *first kidnapped slaves* from Africa to the Americas in 1501. Soon, they were being sent all over the Americas. Many slaves **did not survive** the gruelling journey, as hunger and **DISEASE WERE RIFE** on the overcrowded ships.

Slave traders often bought slaves from African merchants.

How it changed...

The slave trade to the Americas destroyed the lives of more than 12 million Africans before its official end in the 19th century.

the world

Slavery abolished

After centuries of corruption and CRUELTY, America ends slavery

Suffering of slaves

Upon arrival, most slaves worked as farm hands on **PLANTATIONS** – large estates run by wealthy landowners where crops were grown and sold for profit. *Life was miserable*, with slaves made to toil without breaks, or holidays, and **in constant fear**.

Slaves read the Emancipation Proclamation.

Free at last

Slaves in the USA **cast off their chains** in 1863 when President Abraham Lincoln announced the *Emancipation Proclamation*, an order that freed them all. Though no longer owned by someone else, the **PATH TO EQUALITY** for former slaves would not be smooth.

Women get the vote

Women in Britain wage war for the same RIGHT TO VOTE as men

Feminist mission

In 1893, women in New Zealand became the first in the world to be allowed to vote. The idea spread, but in the early 1900s, British women still did not have **SUFFRAGE** (the right to vote) as they were not deemed equal to men. British campaigner Emmeline Pankhurst (above) established the *Women's Social and Political Union* (WSPU) in 1903. A newspaper jokingly named them "**suffragettes**", but the name stuck and the suffragette sisterhood was born.

How it changed...

Equal voting rights allowed women to help shape society. Women are still fighting for equality in other fields today.

the world

The horse was owned by British King George V. It's possible Davison wanted to fix a WSPU scarf to it.

Death at the races

The suffragette motto was "**Deeds, not words**", and women smashed windows, set fire to buildings, and chained themselves to railings to bring attention to the cause. In 1913, British suffragette Emily Davison died after *throwing herself under a horse* at the Epsom Derby horse race. It wasn't clear whether she intended to die or to just cause a scene, but it brought **FURTHER NOTICE** to the WSPU's mission.

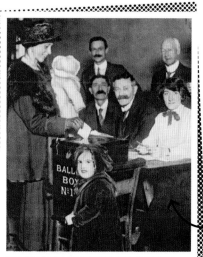

A British woman votes for the first time in the 1918 general election.

Voting victory

Years of campaigning by fearless suffragettes finally paid off. British women were given the **right to vote in 1918**. American women voted by 1920, and many other countries soon followed. Nowadays, **ALL BUT A FEW** countries allow women to vote.

March to Montgomery

Black Americans MARCH for equality

Dream come true

In 1963, Dr Martin Luther King, Jr gave his celebrated "**I HAVE A DREAM**" speech to 250,000 supporters in Washington DC, USA. Calling on the government to help **end racial inequality**, his plea led to the 1964 Civil Rights Act, which banned employers from judging employees on their "**colour, religion, or national origin**".

In the 1950s, racial segregation in the US discriminated against black people, separating them from white people in housing, schooling, and public services. The Civil Rights Movement used campaigns, protests, and marches to bring about equality.

Rosa Parks on a bus after public transport segregation ended.

Bus boycott

A black seamstress from Alabama triggered one of the biggest moments in the **Civil Rights Movement** in 1955 by refusing to give up her seat on a bus to a white man. **ROSA PARKS** was arrested, but civil rights campaigner Dr Martin Luther King, Jr called for his followers to boycott the bus company and *segregation on public transport* ended in 1956.

What came before...

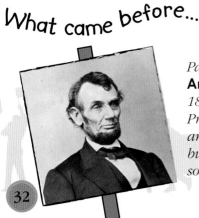

Passed under President **ABRAHAM LINCOLN** *in 1863, the Emancipation Proclamation brought an end to slavery in the USA, but afterwards many states sought to limit its power.*

Indian **MAHATMA GANDHI** *held peaceful protests against British rule in India from the 1930s. Gandhi inspired Dr Martin Luther King, Jr to stage non-violent marches and speeches.*

Vote of confidence

Two years later, King, along with Rosa Parks and other activists, led another march from Selma, Alabama, to the state capital of Montgomery to **protest restrictions on blacks voting**. In spite of *violence* from police along the way, the march resulted in the **VOTING RIGHTS ACT**, which made it easier for black people to vote.

Lasting legacy

Dr Martin Luther King, Jr was killed in 1968 by an assassin opposed to the Civil Rights Movement. Though *relations between the races have not been easy* in the years since, the USA elected its first black president, Barack Obama (above), in 2008. Obama was re-elected in 2012, and swore his presidential oath on a **BIBLE** that was owned by Dr King.

How it changed the world

The Selma to Montgomery March, was one of a handful of events that gave African Americans a voice when they had been silenced by segregation and suffering. Changes in the law meant that black people gained more freedom, but many feel that full equality with whites has still not been achieved.

By the way...

Though I, Rosa Parks, was the most famous bus protestor, Claudette Colvin, who refused to give up her seat nine months before me, was the first.

In 1954, the US Supreme Court declared that schools must provide INTEGRATED EDUCATION for all children, regardless of skin colour.

Civil Rights activists staged PROTESTS in restaurants, swimming pools, and churches, demanding black people be allowed to use these public places.

33

Abolishing apartheid

The mission to stop racial DISCRIMINATION in South Africa

In a troubled time for South Africa, black people endured years of oppression under apartheid (an Afrikaans word meaning "separateness"). Fearless freedom fighters took on their cause and ended up running the country.

Did you know?
Apartheid meant black South Africans had separate schools and couldn't travel where they wanted or marry whites.

Living apart

In 1948, the all-white Afrikaner National Party of South Africa began imposing the system of apartheid on the mostly black country. This **limited what black people could do** and where they could go. It was designed to keep them **APART** from white people, and meant that black people had to live in poor, overcrowded *townships*.

Blacks flee from police bullets at Sharpeville.

Signs like this were once seen everywhere in South Africa.

Protests against prejudice

The black rights group, the **African National Congress (ANC)**, arranged peaceful protests against apartheid. But the organization met with violence many times. One of the worst occasions was the 1960 *Sharpeville Massacre*, when police killed 69 black people. The ANC was banned, and in 1964 one of their leaders, **NELSON MANDELA**, was imprisoned for life.

What came before...

In the late 19th century, European countries raced each other to grab African territory in what was known as the "SCRAMBLE FOR AFRICA".

Quarrels between white settlers in South Africa became violent. In 1880 and again in 1899, war broke out between the British and the BOERS, who were of Dutch and German descent.

End to apartheid

Many countries around the world **put pressure** on South Africa to drop apartheid and release political prisoners like Mandela. While Mandela was still in jail, the South African President, F W de Klerk, *gave in to world pressure*. In 1990, he removed the ban on protest marches and **ENDED APARTHEID**. A new flag was adopted in 1994 that reflected these changes in the country.

The new flag shows the colours of the ANC (green, gold, and black) combining with the blue, white, and red of the country's colonial rulers, Britain and the Netherlands.

By the way...
I received more than 250 awards for my efforts, including the famous Nobel Peace Prize in 1993.

Mandela mania

When apartheid fell, Mandela was released from jail, having served 27 years **behind bars**. He triumphed in South Africa's **FIRST MULTI-RACIAL ELECTION** in 1994 to become the *nation's first black president*.

How it changed the world

Mandela's determination helped to bring about the end of apartheid in South Africa. He advised forgiveness for the wrongs of the past, allowing South Africa to move into a new phase of its history.

What came after...

South Africa's Springboks won the RUGBY WORLD CUP in 1995, and Nelson Mandela wore a team shirt and cap to present the trophy to the captain, Francois Pienaar.

NELSON MANDELA DIED *in 2013 at the age of 95. The world over, people mourned the loss of the "Father of South Africa".*

Humans are an argumentative species. Rivalry, uprisings, and all-out war arose from the time of the first civilizations. From chariot battles over territory and revolutions against rotten rulers, to religious upheaval and the planet-threatening atomic bombs of the 20th century, human conflict has led to some of the most significant changes in world history – for better and for worse.

bust-ups

Egypt v. Hittites

A right royal DUST-UP!

In 1274 BCE, the Egyptians clashed with their rivals, the Hittites. The battle, in a city called Kadesh, was the first conflict in history of which we have a detailed account.

By the way...
I fought in my first military campaign when I was only 14 years old.

Ramses led an Egyptian army of 20,000 men against 50,000 Hittites.

Egypt's rivals

The Hittites were a **warlike people** who had been grabbing territory from Egypt until Pharaoh Ramses II decided to fight back. The Hittites' expert horsemanship and advanced *iron weaponry* made them fearsome warriors. They also prayed to more than **ONE THOUSAND GODS**, including Zababa, the god of war.

Carved head of a Hittite god, found in Barak, Turkey

What came before...

The Egyptians developed one of the earliest forms of writing, called HIEROGLYPHICS, which used pictures and symbols to represent sounds and words. They wrote on wood, paper, and even in stone.

THE HITTITES *originally settled in Anatolia (modern-day Turkey) around 2000 BCE, and soon began to spread south. The city of Hattussa became the Hittite capital and centre of the empire.*

Battle tactics

We know how the battle was fought mainly from Egyptian reports. At first, the Egyptians were **tricked into an ambush**. Then Ramses regrouped and, when his driver was too scared to go back into battle, Ramses **wrapped the chariot horses' reins round his waist** and charged the Hittites, determined to win or **DIE TRYING**.

Egyptian chariots were light and built for two men.

Hittite chariots were bigger and heavier – they could cause more damage but were hard to steer on sand.

Treaty time

Both armies lost a lot of men, and the **battle was a stalemate**. The two sides signed the first surviving **PEACE TREATY**, pledging to share the land and to enter into an alliance. The Hittites **copied the agreement onto clay tablets**, while the Egyptians recorded the details on the walls of temples.

How it changed the world

The dispute between Egypt and the Hittites was eventually settled by an agreement between the two sides. It was the first time that historians know of when peace was achieved through negotiations.

What came after...

RAMSES built a huge temple at **ABU SIMBEL** to mark his victory, even though most historians now agree that there was no clear winner at Kadesh. He ruled for 67 years until his death at the age of 90.

The **HITTITES** believed they had won at Kadesh. They fought the first recorded sea battle in 1210 BCE, against Cyprus. But they were overcome by the rise of the Assyrians, and their empire had collapsed by 1200 BCE.

Caesar takes Rome

From military man to RUTHLESS ruler

In 49 BCE, when Julius Caesar crossed a small river on his way to Rome, it was the first step on his path to becoming the world's most powerful man.

A fighter and a writer

Julius Caesar came from a noble Roman family. Caesar made his name as a **brilliant military general**, but there was much more to him than that. He was also an **ambitious politician**, talented writer, inspiring speaker – and **ADORED BY THE ORDINARY PEOPLE** of Rome.

Did you know?
Caesar was once captured by pirates. He made sure they got well paid for his return, but then he had them executed.

"Rubicon" means "red" – the river appeared reddish due to mud.

What came before...

Rome became a world power because of its **IMPRESSIVE MILITARY MIGHT**. The army was made up of about 30 legions, each containing roughly 5,000 highly trained, well-paid professional soldiers.

Technology developed fast in Rome to meet the needs of the growing empire. Engineers constructed **MAGNIFICENT AQUEDUCTS** to carry water to cities.

The fall of the Gauls

By the age of 40, Caesar was **ELECTED CONSUL**, and formed an alliance with Crassus and Pompey, the two other most powerful men in Rome. He was **hailed as Rome's finest general** after a successful campaign in Gaul (modern-day France). In Rome, the Senate worried that Caesar **wanted to seize power**, and ordered him to disband his army before he returned.

Vercingetorix, the chief of the Gauls, surrendered to Caesar in 52 BCE.

Did you know?
Caesar created the 365-day calendar, which is the basis of the one still used today. "July" is named after him.

Fateful river

An ancient Roman law **forbade generals** with a standing army from crossing the Rubicon river and entering the Roman republic. **Caesar had a choice** – disband the army and stand down, or cross the Rubicon and try to seize power for himself. He bellowed "**THE DIE IS NOW CAST!**" as he crossed the river.

How it changed the world

Caesar's victory over the republicans meant that Rome was now ruled by one person, with power passed on through families. Caesar's heirs would be declared all-powerful emperors, and even worshipped as gods.

Power struggle

Caesar and his army entered Rome and **triggered a fierce war** over who should rule. After years of fighting all over the empire, **Caesar emerged as the winner**. He returned to Rome in triumph and was declared Rome's **DICTATOR FOR LIFE**.

What came after...

In 64 CE, the **GREAT FIRE OF ROME** swept through and destroyed much of the city. The emperor, Nero (left), was blamed by the people for not doing enough to fight the fire or help the victims.

In 313 CE, Constantine became the first Roman emperor to **TOLERATE CHRISTIANITY** and end centuries of Roman brutality to Christians.

The Battle of Hastings

One in the EYE for King Harold

In 1066, Harold Godwinson was crowned king of England, but his rivals, Harald Hardrada and William of Normandy, wanted his crown and were prepared to fight for it.

North and south

First, Norwegian king Hardrada's army **landed near York**, but King Harold's army marched north and defeated the invaders – killing Hardrada with an arrow to the throat. Then the Frenchman William of Normandy landed near **HASTINGS**, 320 km (200 miles) to the south. Harold and his troops rushed to **repel the threat**.

York

Hastings

····▶ William of Normandy's Army
····▶ Hardrada Army
····▶ Harold's Army
◌ Battle

King Harold was killed by an arrow through the eye.

What came before...

Before the Normans arrived, England's people were mainly **ANGLO-SAXONS**, who originally came from Germany and the Netherlands.

THE VIKINGS from Denmark, Norway, and Sweden began frequent raids on England from 793 CE, when they raided a monastery in the northeast of the country.

The battle for England

On Senlac Hill, near Hastings, Harold's army formed a **wall of shields** against the Norman archers. But some of the English broke away from their wall, perhaps to chase retreating Norman soldiers. The Normans *turned back and attacked*. By the end of the Battle of Hastings, Harold was dead and William of Normandy was the **NEW KING OF ENGLAND**.

Did you know?
After his impressive win at the Battle of Hastings, William became known as "The Conqueror".

William fell from his horse during battle, and then lifted his helmet to show his troops that he was still alive.

By the way…
The battle lasted from about 9 am until sundown, and halfway through, both sides took a break for lunch!

How it changed the world

After his victory, William granted most of England's land and many important jobs to his Norman allies. Anglo-Saxon was replaced by Latin as the language of government.

Up to 7,000 men were killed in a day at the Battle of Hastings.

Picture the scene

The huge **BAYEUX TAPESTRY** (above) tells the whole story of the Norman invasion in **72 scenes**. It was worked by William's wife Matilda and her ladies-in-waiting. The tapestry is *70 m (230 ft) long* – the length of seven London buses.

What came after...

William commissioned **THE DOMESDAY BOOK**, *a huge survey of all the land and property in England. It took two years to collect all the information.*

The Normans built massive **STONE CASTLES** *and cathedrals all over England, many of which are still standing.*

The Holy City

By 1095, much of the Middle East, including the holy city of Jerusalem, was controlled by **Muslims**. When **Pope Urban II** received reports of Christians being attacked there, he declared it was every Christian's duty to help each other and to **WIN JERUSALEM BACK** for Christianity. The First Crusade was born.

Pope Urban II asked for help at Clermont, France.

Jerusalem falls

The bloody beginnings of RELIGIOUS WAR for the Holy Land

The Pope hoped knights and other military men would hear his call.

The capturing of Jerusalem was one of the bloodiest episodes of medieval history.

People believed they would go straight to heaven if they died on Crusade.

People's Crusade

Across Europe, people answered the Pope's call. While the knights were still forming an army, the **PEOPLE'S CRUSADE**, made up of peasants, left for Jerusalem. About **40,000 people** set off, but they were **massacred by the Muslims** before reaching the city.

How it changed...

The First Crusade was the start of centuries of struggle for the Holy Land, causing long-lasting bitterness and hatred.

the world

The fall of Jerusalem

The main armies of **knights fought their way** to Jerusalem, arriving in June 1099. After a month of siege, they **BROKE THROUGH THE WALLS**. The crusaders poured into the city and *went on a bloody rampage*, murdering men, women, and children, and stealing everything they found. The Christians had captured Jerusalem, but the Muslims would soon respond.

Universal ruler

In 1206, a young warrior called **Temujin** called the Mongol tribes of eastern Asia together and **PERSUADED THEM TO UNITE**, with him as the leader. He renamed himself *Genghis Khan*, which means "Universal Ruler".

Genghis Khan died in 1227, and was succeeded by his son Ögedei.

Mongols united

How the Mongols came together to CONQUER the world

How it changed...

Though the Mongol empire was short-lived, it made a permanent impact on trade and communication between East and West.

the world

Fearsome fighters

The Mongols were feared wherever they went. Their **SUCCESS** as warriors was based on their *expert horsemanship*, strict discipline, skill with bow and arrow, and the **military genius** of their leaders.

Genghis once executed a foe by pouring molten silver into his eyes and ears.

Russia
ASIA
Mongolia China
Pakistan
AFRICA
Mongol empire 1279

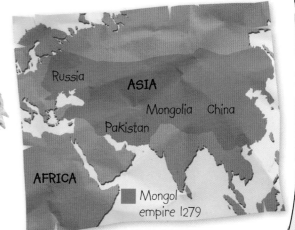

Vast empire

The Mongols were **extremely successful**. Within 50 years of uniting, they ruled **ABOUT 16 PER CENT** of the Earth's land surface, and had claimed 40 million lives as they swept across Asia. But within 50 years, the empire split up, and a century later had *largely disappeared*.

45

The 95 Theses

When a German monk decided to tell the Catholic Church to clean up its act, he sparked a huge protest movement that led to the emergence of Protestantism.

Nailing notices to the door of the local church was a common way of bringing a matter to the local community's attention.

How a one-man religious PROTEST went viral

From lawyer to monk

Martin Luther was born in Germany in 1483. He was studying to be a lawyer when, one day, he was caught in a *violent storm*. The terrified young man prayed to his favourite saint, "If you save me, St Anne, **I'LL BECOME A MONK!**" When Luther escaped unharmed, he kept his promise.

By the way...
I was famous for my bad temper – maybe because I suffered from awful constipation all my life!

St Peter's Basilica in Rome was built mainly with money from Papal Indulgences.

A Church gone bad

After many years, Luther came to feel that the Catholic Church had gone astray. Many priests were **LAZY AND CORRUPT**. The head of the Church, the Pope, raised money by selling "*Papal Indulgences*" – a system where people gave money to the Pope and, in return, he **forgave their sins**, on behalf of God. Luther wanted the Church to set a better example.

What came before...

In 1054, the **CHRISTIAN CHURCH SPLIT**. *The Roman Catholic Church in the West was ruled by the Pope. The eastern Greek Orthodox Church was led by the Patriarch of Constantinople.*

The pope who excommunicated Luther, Leo X (left), was from the rich and powerful **MEDICI FAMILY** *of Florence, Italy. The family produced a total of four popes and two queens of France.*

Hammer time

On 31 October 1517, Luther **nailed a notice** to the door of the Church in Wittenberg, listing the 95 things he believed were wrong with the Church. The Pope and other *Church leaders were furious*, but many people agreed with Luther. His "**95 THESES**" were translated from Latin and distributed all over Germany. Luther had started a religious revolution!

John Calvin created a strict version of Protestantism at his church in Geneva, Switzerland.

How it changed the world

Though he only set out to reform the Church, Luther's actions led to a new type of Christianity called Protestantism, which 800 million people worldwide follow today. The 95 Theses led to the era of religious upheaval we call the Reformation.

Reform spreads

Luther was excommunicated (banned) from the Church and declared an outlaw. He **WENT INTO HIDING**, but was protected by his local prince, Frederick the Wise. He continued to speak out against the Church, and, alongside other reformers, such as Frenchman **John Calvin and John Knox** from Scotland, he began to lay the foundations for the Protestant branch of Christianity, which took root in northern Europe.

What came after...

Arguments over the Reformation led to the **THIRTY YEARS' WAR** *(1618–1648). During the conflict, Germany lost up to 40 per cent of its population, and a third of its towns were destroyed.*

In England, the Reformation began when King **HENRY VIII** *divorced his wife, was excommunicated by the Pope, and set himself up as head of the new Church of England.*

47

Aztecs and Incas defeated

Two great civilizations DESTROYED by fortune hunters

When the Spanish landed in the Americas, they found civilizations that had flourished for centuries. But within a few decades, those ancient cultures had been wiped out by the newcomers.

Treasure hunters

When explorer **Christopher Columbus** returned to Spain in 1493 with tales of the treasures he had seen in the Americas, other **SPANISH ADVENTURERS** were tempted to see for themselves. They set sail *in search of wealth*, especially gold.

The Spanish were called "conquistadors" – which means "conquerors".

Cortés and Moctezuma

Spaniard **HERNAN CORTÉS** landed in Mexico in 1519, with an army of 600 men. When he was brought to *Moctezuma II, leader of the Aztecs*, he was welcomed with lavish gifts. Things deteriorated, however, when Cortés **took Moctezuma hostage** and made himself governor. Moctezuma was killed soon after.

What came before...

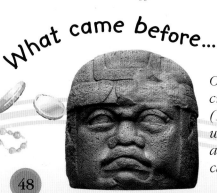

One of the earliest American civilizations, the **OLMECS** (1200–400 BCE) were farmers who also produced striking artwork, including giant, carved stone heads.

THE MAYA (400 BCE–1697 CE) of Central America devised a form of writing and made books, called codices, which told stories about Maya life and mythology.

Moctezuma possibly welcomed Cortés because an Aztec prophecy foretold the arrival of a god with white skin.

After his capture, Atahualpa converted to Christianity and was renamed Francisco Atahualpa, after Pizarro.

The fall of the Inca

In 1532, conquistador **FRANCISCO PIZARRO** destroyed the other great civilization of Latin America, the Inca. Pizarro *took the Inca king Atahualpa hostage* and, although the Incas paid a huge ransom of gold, **Pizarro had Atahualpa strangled** and seized control of Inca lands and treasure.

How it changed the world

The destruction of the ancient American cultures paved the way for a huge wave of settlers from Spain to South America. Today, most South American countries are Spanish-speaking and have strong ties with Spain.

Neither the Spanish nor the Aztecs claimed responsibility for Moctezuma's death.

Spanish success

The conquistadors defeated the Aztecs and Incas mainly because they had **HORSES AND GUNS**. The Spanish also brought *illnesses such as smallpox and flu*. Thousands of native people died because they had **no immunity** to these European diseases.

Smallpox was very contagious. It caused fever and blisters, and often led to death.

What came after...

BARTOLOMÉ DE LAS CASAS (1474–1566) was a priest who campaigned for the rights of the Native American slaves, who were brutally treated by the Spanish settlers.

The Spanish **SPREAD CHRISTIANITY** throughout their colonies. Today, more than 40 per cent of the world's Catholics live in Latin America.

The siege of Vienna

When Vienna said "nein!" to the mighty OTTOMAN empire

By the 1500s, the Ottoman Turks ruled the Middle East and most of eastern Europe. But when they headed west to take the city of Vienna in 1529, it all started to go wrong...

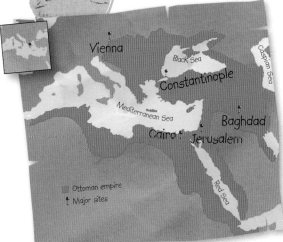

Islamic conquerors

The Ottoman empire was **FOUNDED IN ANATOLIA** (modern-day Turkey) in about 1300 by an *Islamic warrior called Osman*. In just over 200 years, it had become one of the **world's most powerful empires**, thanks to its superior military and infighting in the lands they conquered.

Suleiman the Magnificent

Suleiman I was the **tenth Ottoman sultan**. He was a brilliant general who personally led his troops into battle and he was also a **POET, ART-LOVER, AND GOLDSMITH**, who spoke five languages. The Ottoman empire reached its furthest extent during his 46-year rule, and by 1529 Vienna stood in the way of its *expansion into western Europe*.

Did you know?
Throughout its 600-year history, the Ottoman empire was ruled by sultans who were all descendants of the same family.

Suleiman's reign was the longest of any sultan.

What came before...

In 1200, Vienna built **FORTRESS-LIKE CITY WALLS**, to keep out invaders. In 1485, the Hungarians laid siege to Vienna for six months, until the citizens were forced to surrender.

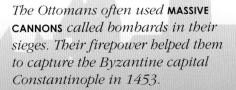

The Ottomans often used **MASSIVE CANNONS** called bombards in their sieges. Their firepower helped them to capture the Byzantine capital Constantinople in 1453.

The siege of Vienna

Suleiman mustered his **vast army** in Bulgaria and set off, but rainy weather turned the route to mud and **Suleiman lost many guns, camels, and even men** on the way. When they finally laid siege to Vienna, more rain and snow and a lack of supplies spelt **DISASTER FOR THE OTTOMANS**. They gave up and began the long journey home.

City defenders

The Ottoman defeat was also partly down to the **courageous defence** of Vienna. Farmers, peasants, and civilians came together and constructed defences to protect their city. The famous German **LANDSKNECHT** soldiers also *put their lives on the line* in an heroic effort.

The Landsknechts were famed for their fighting skills and colourful clothes.

How it changed the world

Vienna was the conflict that proved the Ottomans were not unstoppable. The Christian nations of Europe began a gradual push back, and from 1529 Ottoman power began to steadily decline.

What came after...

In 1683, the Ottomans failed again to take Vienna. Legend has it that the Viennese celebrated by baking pastries that mimicked the crescent symbol on the Ottoman flag. We know them today as CROISSANTS*!*

Ottoman rule came to an end when the last sultan, Mehmet VI, was forced to abdicate in 1922. A year later, the modern state of **TURKEY** *was founded by army officer Kemal Atatürk.*

American War of Independence

A new country explodes into life

In 1775, unrest in the 13 American colonies over British rule spilled over into revolution, and a war for American independence began.

The British are coming!

In April 1775, **PAUL REVERE** (right), an American who belonged to a rebel group called the Sons of Liberty, was **spying on British troops** stationed in Boston. When he saw that the British were ready to move on American rebels gathered in the city of Lexington, Massachusetts, he **rode all through the night** to warn rebel commanders throughout the state. The war was about to begin!

The first battles

When the British reached Lexington on 19 April, **the rebels were ready**. During a small skirmish, shots were fired. The first shot was famously described by American poet Ralph Waldo Emerson as the "**SHOT HEARD AROUND THE WORLD**" as it meant war had begun. Later that day, at Concord, the first proper battle was **won by the rebels**, forcing the British to retreat to Boston.

What led to it...

The British imposed **HEAVY TAXES** on the American colonists. The taxes were unpopular, especially since the colonists couldn't vote in the British parliament.

In 1773, during the **BOSTON TEA PARTY**, rebels boarded British ships and dumped their cargo of tea into Boston harbour.

Declaration of Independence

As the fighting wore on, the 13 rebel American colonies decided to **form their own government** (Congress). Thomas Jefferson, a lawyer, wrote the **DECLARATION OF INDEPENDENCE** for the new nation and presented it to Congress. On 4 July 1776, *the United States of America* (USA) was born.

By the way...
As well as being a fast rider and an American hero, I was also a silversmith, a book illustrator, and a part-time dentist.

General Charles O'Hara surrendered on behalf of the British on 19 October 1781.

Did you know?
Paul Revere's ride only became famous 95 years after the event, when poet Henry Longfellow wrote a poem about it.

The Declaration was signed by 56 members of Congress.

Victory in Yorktown

War raged for eight years, until the Americans, helped by the French navy, surrounded the British army in the **PORT OF YORKTOWN**. After a 21-day siege, the 8,000 **British troops surrendered**. Britain realized it was losing the war, and *suggested peace talks*. The rebels had won.

How it changed the world

The colonists fought the war over their stated belief that all men are created free and equal, and have the same natural rights. This idea helped shape the way people all over the world thought about human rights, and democracy.

What came after...

After the war, the commander of the American army, **GEORGE WASHINGTON,** *was hailed a hero – and in 1789 he was elected the first president of the USA.*

The French Revolution

When the King of France lost his HEAD

In 1789, French revolutionaries dreamed of creating a fairer, more decent country – but the dream soon turned into a nightmare of bloodshed and chaos.

By the way...
At the fairy-tale farm I had built at Versailles, I pretended to be a shepherdess, tending to a flock of perfumed sheep and lambs!

The mob killed the governor of the Bastille, then paraded his head through the streets on a spike.

Rich and poor

In the 18th century, the nobles and churchmen of France enjoyed huge wealth and privilege, while *ordinary people went hungry*. King Louis XVI and his queen, **MARIE ANTOINETTE** (above), were caught between pleasing the different groups, and ended up angering them all. As time passed, people grew **impatient with the king**.

The people are revolting

Unrest turned to revolution on **14 JULY 1789**, when an angry mob rampaged through Paris and **broke into the Bastille fortress**. They freed the seven prisoners inside and, more importantly, seized the huge stocks of *weapons and gunpowder* stored there. Revolution had begun.

What came before...

The Enlightenment was a time in the 1700s when people began to challenge traditional ways of thinking. French philosopher **VOLTAIRE** *said that all people should have freedom of speech.*

For centuries, France had been divided into **THREE CLASSES, OR ESTATES***: churchmen, nobility, and common people. The first two estates enjoyed many privileges and huge wealth.*

Off with their heads!

By 1791, the **revolutionaries ruled France**. They passed laws to make society more equal, and to *reduce the power of the Church and nobility*. King Louis XVI and Queen Marie Antoinette tried to escape from France in disguise, but they were captured, imprisoned, and eventually **BEHEADED** by the guillotine for treason in 1793.

By July 1794, everyone was sick of Robespierre's brutality. He was himself executed, to the cheers of the people of Paris.

The guillotine was designed to make death quick and (relatively!) painless.

Charles-Henri Sanson executed the King. He executed about 3,000 people during his career.

Robespierre's Terror

Radical lawyer **MAXIMILIEN ROBESPIERRE** became one of the most powerful figures of the Revolution. He was responsible for the **Reign of Terror** of 1793–1794, when up to *40,000 French people were executed* or died in prison, sometimes just because Robespierre suspected they were against the Revolution.

Did you know?
Louis was stripped of all his royal titles and executed under his birth name of "Louis Capet".

How it changed the world

The leaders of the French Revolution put forward ideas about freedom, equality, and democracy that eventually spread all over Europe and vastly improved the lives of ordinary people.

What came after...

After the Revolution collapsed in 1799, a brilliant soldier called **NAPOLEON BONAPARTE** rose up to became a military hero, and, in 1804, emperor of France.

Napoleon wanted to rule Europe, but he was defeated in 1815 at Waterloo by the British, led by the **DUKE OF WELLINGTON** (right). Napoleon fell from power and died in 1821.

American revolutions

How a young rebel led SIX different uprisings against Spanish rule!

After 300 years of being ruled by Spain, by 1810, the people of South America had had enough. They wanted independence, and they were prepared to fight for it!

Napoleon's brother was crowned Joseph I

Trigger for rebellion

By 1800, much of South America was under **Spanish control**. Then, when Emperor Napoleon of France **invaded Spain** and made his brother king, the Spanish were furious. The South American colonies saw a chance to go for **INDEPENDENCE** while the Spanish were distracted by troubles at home.

What came after...

In 1810, Mexican priest **MIGUEL HIDALGO** led a rebellion with his cry of "Viva Mexico!" Mexico finally declared independence in 1821.

In 1817, rebels **BERNARDO O'HIGGINS** (left), José de San Martin, and 5,000 men trekked over the Andes to surprise Spanish troops at the Battle of Chacabuco, and liberated Chile.

Young revolutionary

Simon Bolívar was a Venezuelan who, inspired by the revolutions in France and America, vowed to free his country from Spanish rule. Bolívar and his followers *invaded Venezuela on 14 May 1813* and although he was hailed by the people as *El Libertador* (the **LIBERATOR**), civil war meant he had to flee. He returned and finished the job in 1821.

Busy liberator

Bolívar wasn't only a hero **AT HOME IN VENEZUELA**, where they named their currency, **the Bolivar**, after him in 1879. He also *helped to liberate Ecuador*, Colombia, Peru, Panama, and Bolivia, which they then named after him, too. He died in 1830 of tuberculosis.

How it changed the world

After the revolutions, Europe had lost virtually all its lands in North and South America, plus the valuable natural resources that went with them. Although Europe still dominated trade around the world, it would never rule so much of the planet again.

In 1821, **José de San Martin** *invaded Peru, which was the centre of Spanish rule in South America, and declared independence.*

In 1825, after 16 years of struggle led by **Antonio José de Sucre**, *Bolivia declared independence from Spain.*

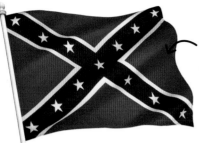

The battle flag of the Confederacy came to be the main symbol of the Southern states.

The Confederacy

When **Abraham Lincoln** was elected president of the USA in 1861, 11 Southern states broke away to form their own nation, **the Confederacy**. They worried that Lincoln might interfere in their laws and restrict **SLAVERY**. The other states, known as the Union, decided to stop them. The USA was at war – with itself.

Gettysburg Address

A SPEECH that rallied the Unionists in the US Civil War

The speech

After the war's deadliest battle at Gettysburg, President **Lincoln made a speech** on 19 November 1863 that reminded people they were fighting for the **future of the Union and the meaning of liberty**. Though only 271 words long, Lincoln's **GETTYSBURG ADDRESS** became a rallying cry that strengthened the Unionists' determination to win the war.

During the Civil War, 2 per cent of the US population died. This is equivalent to six million men today.

The South burns

Gradually, Lincoln's **UNIONIST ARMY** gained the upper hand. He freed the slaves in 1863, and many black men fought on the Union side. The Union army marched through the South, **burning the land** as they went. Finally, in April 1865, the **Confederates surrendered**. The war was over.

How it changed... United and determined never to fight each other again, the USA quickly grew to be the richest, most powerful nation in the world. **the world**

Settlers spread west

In the 19th century, the USA was rapidly expanding. White **SETTLERS WENT WEST** in search of new territory, to the lands of the *Native Americans* who had always lived there. Many tribes were forced off their own land and into areas called **reservations**.

Battle of Little Bighorn

Custer's final fight, and one of the last for NATIVE AMERICANS

Trouble brewing

As time passed, the Natives were *forced onto ever-smaller reservations*, and whites often **INTRUDED** even on these meagre lands. Angered by this, the Natives, led by Hunkpapa chief Sitting Bull, decided to **fight back**. In response, the US army sent a cavalry division led by Civil War veteran George Custer.

A Native reservation

Custer was called "Yellow Hair" and "Son of the Morning Star" by the Natives.

Custer's last stand

Surprised by a *larger force than expected*, Custer's unit was cornered by a river called **Little Bighorn**. Custer and all 210 of his men were killed. The Natives couldn't celebrate for long, as the US army responded with more soldiers. Within a year, many of the Natives had **SURRENDERED**, and Sitting Bull had fled to Canada.

How it changed...

Little Bighorn was the tribes' last triumph. By the 20th century, white settlers had claimed almost all of North America.

the world

Assassinations

The unlucky leaders who met a TRAGIC end as they tried to change the world

The Senate was the place where the rulers of Rome met to debate and pass laws.

Julius Caesar

By 44 BCE, **Roman war hero Julius Caesar** was the most powerful man in the world. He had been made "Dictator for Life" of Rome, in charge of its vast empire. But some Romans felt that this was too much power for one man, so they **PLOTTED TO KILL** him. On 15 March 44 BCE, when Caesar arrived at the Senate, he was *surrounded by a group of Senators*. They unsheathed their daggers and stabbed him 23 times until he fell, dead, onto the Senate floor.

Did you know?
While escaping after shooting President Lincoln, the killer fell off the theatre stage and broke his leg.

Abraham Lincoln

Abraham Lincoln was president of the USA from 1861 to 1865. He led the country during the American Civil War, when some states, who called themselves the Confederacy, fought against Lincoln's policy to **RESTRICT SLAVERY**. After four years, Lincoln's side won, but just a week later the *president was shot dead* while he and his wife were watching a play at the theatre. The killer was an actor and Confederacy spy called John Wilkes Booth, who was shot dead himself 11 days later.

Mohandas "Mahatma" Gandhi

Indian lawyer **Mohandas Gandhi** was famous for his **NON-VIOLENT CAMPAIGNS AGAINST INJUSTICE**. He led the successful fight for Indian independence from Britain by staging hunger strikes and sit-down protests, disobeying unfair laws, or refusing to work. In 1948, he was *killed at a prayer meeting* by a religious fanatic who opposed Gandhi's work to bring Muslims and Hindus together.

The nickname "Mahatma" means "Great Soul".

John F. Kennedy

When 43-year-old **John Fitzgerald Kennedy** was elected president of the USA in 1960, he was the youngest man ever to be elected to the job. But three years later, on 22 November 1963, the popular president was **SHOT DEAD IN DALLAS, TEXAS**, while riding in an open-top car. The assassination deeply shocked people all over the world. An ex-US marine called *Lee Harvey Oswald* was arrested for the killing, but he himself was shot and killed before he could stand trial.

Did you know?
There are at least 730 streets in the USA named after Martin Luther King, Jr.

Martin Luther King, Jr

Martin Luther King, Jr was an African-American campaigner for equal rights. He organized massive, **NON-VIOLENT PROTESTS**, and made inspiring speeches. He helped to introduce laws that made sure all Americans were treated equally at school, and in their jobs. King was **shot dead in 1968**, at a hotel in Memphis, Tennessee. A small-time criminal called James Earl Ray *confessed to the murder* and was sentenced to 99 years in jail.

King had survived an assassination attempt in 1958, when Izola Curry stabbed him in the chest with a letter opener.

Franz Ferdinand assassinated

How the pulling of a trigger set off a global WAR

Franz Ferdinand died from a single gunshot wound to his neck.

In 1914, tempers in Europe were short as different countries picked quarrels with each other. When the heir to the throne of Austria-Hungary was murdered in Sarajevo, the built-up tension boiled over into all-out war.

In Treue feſt!

German ruler Kaiser Wilhelm II (left), and Austria's Emperor Franz Joseph were staunch allies.

Divided Europe

Fierce rivalry between European countries for trade and territory had created a hostile atmosphere, with **two alliance systems** at work. Germany, Austria, and Italy worked together, with Britain, France, and Russia declaring each other allies. The German ruler, Kaiser Wilhelm II, wanted to make his country a world power. When *he built up a formidable navy*, both France and Britain were alarmed by the **KAISER'S AGGRESSION**.

What came after...

At the **BATTLE OF GALLIPOLI**, in 1915, the British and their allies suffered huge casualties fighting against Turkey, which sided with Germany.

During the five-month **BATTLE OF THE SOMME** in France, in 1916, more than a million soldiers were killed. Britain lost about 20,000 men on the first day alone.

Assassination at Sarajevo

On 28 June 1914, Austria-Hungary's **Archduke Franz Ferdinand** was visiting the Serbian city of **SARAJEVO**. Protestors threw a bomb at the Archduke's motorcade, but he survived. Then, later, another member of the gang spotted the Archduke in his car. He *fired his gun*, killing both Franz Ferdinand and his wife, Sophie.

On the Western Front, men on both sides were bogged down in muddy trenches. Tens of thousands died in every battle.

The world at war

Within a month, an angry Austria-Hungary, supported by their German allies, had **DECLARED WAR ON SERBIA**. Within days, the two main alliances had declared war on each other and combat began. In 1917, the United States joined in against Germany. What we now know as World War I was **fought on two main fronts**: the Western in Belgium and northern France, and the Eastern in Russia. For the first time, *tanks and aeroplanes* were used in combat.

Did you know?
The assassin, Gavrilo Princip, was a member of a gang of Bosnians who wanted freedom from Austria-Hungary.

How it changed the world

Franz Ferdinand's death started the largest conflict the world had ever seen. By its end in 1918, 20 million people would be dead and the map of Europe completely redrawn.

The war lasted for four years, until Germany, short of supplies and men and deserted by its allies, **ASKED FOR A CEASEFIRE** *in November 1918.*

Everyone was hard up after the war. In Germany, the price of goods rose out of control and people found that their **MONEY WAS WORTH ALMOST NOTHING.**

Atomic bombs dropped

A devastating end to World War II

When US scientists found a way to create deadly weapons by splitting atoms, it resulted in two bomb attacks that sent shockwaves around the world.

A long, hard war

In April 1945, **GERMANY** finally surrendered, ending six long years of World War II in Europe. But in the Pacific, the fight against Germany's partner, Japan, dragged on. US military commanders calculated that it would *cost them up to a million soldiers' lives* to invade Japan. Instead, they decided on another way to end the war – by developing atomic bombs, the **most devastating weapons** the world had ever seen.

The temperature at the centre of the Hiroshima bomb explosion was three times hotter than the core of the Sun.

Soviet troops raise the USSR flag over the German Reichstag (parliament) in Berlin.

Atomic arms race

In the US, the secret **wartime scheme** to develop an atomic bomb was code-named the *Manhattan Project*. The head scientist, **J ROBERT OPPENHEIMER**, was helped by a team of scientists, many of whom had fled to the USA from Nazi-occupied Europe.

What came before...

Times 1d
AUGUST 5, 1914
BRITAIN AT WAR

In September 1939, Adolf Hitler, Nazi dictator of Germany, invaded Poland. This broke an agreement he had made with Britain and France, who DECLARED WAR.

During the war, the Nazis executed SIX MILLION JEWISH PEOPLE from all over Europe. This systematic murder is now known as the Holocaust.

Weapon of mass destruction

The bombs Oppenheimer's team developed were nicknamed **Little Boy and Fat Man**. Little Boy was 3 m (10 ft) long and **weighed the same as an adult elephant**. Its destructive power came from reactions within atoms, which is why it was called an **ATOMIC BOMB** (and sometimes, a nuclear bomb). Fat Man was slightly larger and 40 per cent more lethal.

Little Boy was fitted with a parachute to slow its drop and allow time for the plane to escape the blast zone.

Did you know?
There were about 165 known "double survivors" – people who experienced both atomic bombs.

How it changed the world

Though the atomic bombs ended the worst conflict in human history, they also showed humans just how destructive war could be. In the following years, other countries developed their own atomic bombs, but the fear of them being used has kept the Western world largely free from major wars.

Hiroshima and Nagasaki

On 6 August 1945, the USA dropped Little Boy on the Japanese **CITY OF HIROSHIMA**. More than 70,000 people were killed instantly, and twice that number died later, as a result of radiation. Three days later, Fat Man was dropped on **Nagasaki**, again causing *devastation and horrific suffering*. Japan surrendered, and World War II was finally over.

Invading the Soviet Union turned out to be Hitler's biggest mistake. His long campaign to take the CITY OF STALINGRAD ended in failure and the loss of 850,000 men.

On 6 June 1944 (D-Day), British, American, and Allied troops landed on the BEACHES OF NORTHERN FRANCE, and began gradually to win mainland Europe back from German control.

Cuban Missile Crisis

When the world came close to TOTAL WIPEOUT

After World War II, the allies USA and USSR became rival superpowers, and by the 1960s, both had nuclear weapons. A stand-off on a tiny island in the Pacific called Cuba brought the world close to nuclear destruction.

Cracks appear

The splits between the USSR, led by Josef Stalin and the UK (led by Winston Churchill) and USA (led by Franklin D Roosevelt) *appeared before the end of World War II*, as they disagreed over how to deal with postwar Europe. The **USSR wanted more territory**, but the Americans feared more countries in Europe turning **COMMUNIST** under Soviet influence.

Churchill (left) and Roosevelt (middle) didn't trust Stalin (right).

US President John F Kennedy appeared on television on 22 October 1962 to explain that nuclear missiles had been spotted in Cuba.

Arms race

Instead of **going to war**, the USA and USSR put their energies into developing more and more **NUCLEAR MISSILES**. The weapons' awesome power meant neither side could afford to launch an attack as a war would *destroy themselves as well as the enemy*. The weapons sat aimed at each other on permanent standby.

What came before...

When civil war broke out in **KOREA IN 1950**, the USA supported South Korea, while the USSR backed the communists in the North.

The USA and its allies formed the military organization **NATO**. In response, the USSR and its allies created the Warsaw Pact.

Crisis in Cuba

In October 1962, US President John F Kennedy found out that the USSR had **SECRETLY** stationed missiles on the island of Cuba, only 150 km (90 miles) from US territory. The weapons pointed towards the USA, and were capable of *causing mass destruction*. Kennedy demanded that Soviet leader Nikita Khrushchev remove them. Khrushchev refused. **The world held its breath**.

Fidel Castro led a communist revolution in Cuba in 1959, and became an ally of the USSR soon after.

Nikita Khrushchev was the Soviet leader from 1953–1964.

Cuba was blockaded by President Kennedy, to stop Soviet ships from transporting missiles to the island.

Crisis averted

The Cuban Missile Crisis ended after 13 nervy days when the **USSR** agreed to take back the missiles. Both sides *signed a treaty* that limited their weapon building. They also installed a **telephone "hotline"** so that leaders of the USA and USSR could be in direct contact.

How it changed the world

The world had come so close to a disastrous nuclear war during the Cuban Missile Crisis that the USA and USSR tried hard afterwards to avoid direct confrontation with each other. Instead, they competed in other areas, such as space exploration, and supported different sides in conflicts and uprisings.

What came after...

CZECHOSLOVAKIA *was a communist country heavily propped up by the USSR. In 1968, an anti-communist uprising was violently put down by Soviet troops.*

*The Soviets and the USA backed opposite sides when communist **NORTH VIETNAM** broke away from the South in 1955, sparking 20 years of war.*

The Fall of the Wall

Decades of DIVISION between East and West Germany end

In 1961, the Berlin Wall was built to prevent East Germans fleeing out of the city to the West. Its destruction 28 years later marked the end of communism in Europe.

Berliners began to demolish the wall once the East German government fell.

Divided Deutschland

After **WORLD WAR II**, Germany was divided into *communist East Germany* and democratic West Germany. The city of **Berlin was also divided**, with the western part controlled by the USA, France, and Britain, and the eastern zone by the Soviet Union (USSR).

Berlin

East Germany

West Germany

East Berlin

West Berlin

What came before...

THE **USSR** *fought anti-communist rebels in Afghanistan from 1979–1989. The war was costly and left the Soviet economy in deep trouble.*

Separated families

East Germany needed to stop people from leaving to live in the West. Overnight, the USSR built a **HUGE WALL ACROSS BERLIN**. Armed guards *shot at anyone* who tried to get over the wall. People were shocked to find out they were stuck on one side or the other, **cut off from family** and friends.

End of communism

In 1989, **Soviet leader Mikhail Gorbachev** decided that the USSR could no longer afford to prop up the other communist governments in Eastern Europe, and, one by one, these **regimes were overthrown**. The East German government fell in November, and people on both sides rushed to tear down the **HATED BERLIN WALL**.

By the way...
A year after the wall fell, East and West Germany became one country again, with a reunited Berlin as the capital.

Mikhail Gorbachev received the Nobel Peace Prize in 1990 for helping to end the Cold War.

How it changed the world

The fall of the Berlin Wall marked the beginning of the end of the Cold War, which had divided the world and threatened peace since the end of World War II.

The wall today

Parts of the wall have been left standing, as a **memorial** to the estimated **136 PEOPLE WHO DIED** trying to cross it. The wall is also a vivid reminder of the bitter divisions that *split the world* for almost 30 years.

What came after...

Romania was one of the last communist regimes in Eastern Europe. Brutal dictator NICOLAE CEAUSESCU led the country for 25 years before he was overthrown.

IN DECEMBER 1991, the USSR broke up into 15 separate countries. The largest of the new states was the Russian Federation, which adopted this flag.

Troubling times

When things go wrong, the effects can be long-lasting. These events caused trouble for a lot of people. Some of the PROBLEMS have been solved, others haven't.

Irish Taoiseach Bertie Ahern, US Senator George Mitchell, and British Prime Minister Tony Blair during the Good Friday Agreement talks.

The Northern Irish Troubles

In the late 1960s, violence erupted in **Northern Ireland** as the ruling British and their supporters clashed with political groups who *wanted a united Ireland*. The conflict came to be known as "The Troubles", and ended in 1998 when peace talks resulted in the **GOOD FRIDAY AGREEMENT**. The agreement was signed by England, Northern Ireland, and the Republic of Ireland, and has largely brought peace and reduced tension in the region.

Did you know?
After peace talks to end the Israeli-Palestinian conflict broke down, a second *intifada* was called in 2000.

Palestinian *intifada*

The *intifada* (meaning "*shaking off*") of 1987 was an uprising by Palestinian rebels against what they saw as the Israeli occupation of their lands. In the **long conflict** that followed, more than 2,000 people were killed and tens of thousands injured. **PEACE TALKS** have been attempted, but haven't yet eased the situation.

9/11

On 11 September 2001, four ordinary American passenger planes were **hijacked** by members of an extremist Islamic group known as al-Qaeda. The **TERRORISTS** flew two of the planes straight into the twin towers of the World Trade Center in New York. Another plane hit the headquarters of the Department of Defence, the Pentagon, in Washington DC, and the fourth crashed in a field. *Around 3,000 people died*.

Terrorist planes hit the Twin Towers.

Flames rise in the streets of Cairo, Egypt, during the Arab Spring.

Did you know?
After 9/11, the US declared a "War on Terror" – which led to wars in Afghanistan and Iraq.

Protests on Wall Street, New York's financial district.

Global banking crisis

In 2008, an **economic crisis** began in the USA, where banks lent a lot of money to people who couldn't pay it back. The banks themselves had to borrow to survive. Soon, no one dared lend anybody anything. World *cash flow dried up*, and many people lost their homes and jobs as a result of the crisis, leading to a widening gap between the **RICH AND THE POOR**.

Arab Spring

Starting in December 2010, a wave of *protests and civil wars* spread across the Arab world. The people of Tunisia, Libya, Egypt, and Yemen forced their longstanding dictators out of power. There were **UPRISINGS** in many other Arab countries, as ordinary citizens made it plain that they would not accept bad government. The whole revolution was called the "Arab Spring", suggesting a time of **new beginnings**. The chain of events set in motion continues today, but not all changes have lasted.

All

History tends to move at a very slow pace, with changes happening over time and in unnoticeable ways. Every now and then, however, a single event clearly marks the beginning of a new era, where things will never be quite the same again. It might be the rise or fall of an empire, an extraordinary personality who seizes the moment, or even a completely random incident. Whether they are moments of triumph or tragedy, some events are so powerful that they change the world forever, often in unforeseeable ways.

By the way...
I'm Cicero! I was a writer, lawyer, and philosopher, but did you know I was a Roman consul, too? I had several run-ins with Julius Caesar...

Kingdom to republic

Rome's legendary first king was its founder **ROMULUS** who, along with his twin brother Remus, had been *raised by a wolf*. Romulus killed Remus after a squabble about where to build the city, and then made himself Rome's first king. The last king, **Tarquin the Proud**, was overthrown in 509 BCE for being... too proud.

Romulus and Remus

Senators served for life.

Ruling the republic

After Tarquin was toppled, Rome was a republic (ruled by its people) for 500 years. All free men had the right to vote. They elected two **CONSULS** to run Rome, helped by the **Senate**. In difficult times, consuls might appoint a *dictator* to lead on their behalf, and make all the decisions.

Roman Republic is founded

One of the world's SUPER STATES started as a tiny kingdom in 753 BCE

How it changed...

In its time as a republic, Rome's armies made it a world power, conquering provinces on three continents.

the world

Republic to empire

Wars of conquest brought Rome power and riches. **Julius Caesar** was one of the last dictators. Civil wars led to the *collapse of the republic* in 27 BCE after which Rome became an empire. Caesar's adopted son **AUGUSTUS** was its first emperor.

Rome's first emperor, Augustus, shown on a coin

Alaric was born in what is now Romania.

The sack of Rome

How BARBARIANS brought the world's greatest empire to its knees

Barbarians seize their chance

In 286 CE, the Roman emperor Diocletian split the Roman empire in two because it was too big to govern alone. Seeing an opportunity, *Germanic tribes* (known to the Romans as "barbarians"), such as the Goths and the Vandals, soon targeted the weaker, western half. In 376, the Goths pushed into Roman territory, and in 410 **ALARIC**, king of the **Visigoths**, looted Rome itself. Vandal raiders sacked the city again in 455. Rome was weakening.

When Alaric died, the Visigoths hid his grave by diverting a river, burying him in the channel, and then diverting the river back over his grave.

Odoacer knocking off Romulus's crown

End of an empire

The last Roman emperor in the west, **Romulus Augustulus**, was just a boy. He was overthrown in 476 CE by a "barbarian" leader called **ODOACER**. Slowly, different peoples took over the western lands. The eastern half of the empire, *Byzantium*, survived for another thousand years.

How it changed...

There was instability in Europe for a time, but slowly, new kingdoms emerged and the medieval age began.

the world

Alexander destroys Persepolis

How a king from a small GREEK city-state built a mighty EMPIRE

In 331 BCE, the Macedonian king and general Alexander the Great defeated Darius III and took control of the mighty Persian empire. Here's how…

From king to pharaoh

Macedonia was just a Greek city-state when Alexander became king in 336 BCE. After pumping up his kingdom's status in Greece, Alexander set out to **build an empire**. He swept undefeated across Asia Minor (modern-day Turkey), Syria, and **EGYPT**. Once there, he gave himself a grand new title – pharaoh!

Alexander founded the port of Alexandria in Egypt.

Alexander was only 25 when he ruined Persepolis!

What came after...

General **PERDICCAS** ruled Macedonia as regent for Alexander's son Alexander IV, who was born in August 323 BCE. Perdiccas was assassinated two or three years later.

General Ptolemy I Soter took over Alexander's kingdom of Egypt. He founded a dynasty that ruled for almost 300 years. The last Ptolemaic pharaoh was clever **CLEOPATRA** (left).

Old enemies

Alexander's sights were set on the *Persian empire*. The Greeks had never forgiven King Xerxes for invading and burning Athens in 480 BCE. Alexander defeated **DARIUS III** (Xerxes's great-great-great-great-grandson) at the **Battle of Issus** in 333 BCE and then again, once and for all, at the Battle of Gaugamela in 331 BCE.

Xerxes humiliated the Greeks during the Greco-Persian wars.

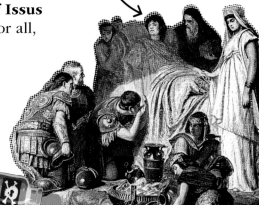

Alexander died at the age of 32 in the palace of Nebuchadnezzar II of Babylon.

Perfect revenge

Next, Alexander moved on to **PERSEPOLIS**, the Persian capital. Most of its palaces and fine buildings had been completed during **Xerxes's reign**. Alexander instructed his men to kill every last Persian, loot the city's treasures, and *torch its buildings*. Much of Persepolis was burned to the ground, just as the Greek capital, Athens, had been in 480 BCE.

By the way…
Alexander's boyhood tutor was the ancient Greek philosopher Aristotle.

Sudden end

Alexander marched his men as far as India, but then they refused to go any further. They returned to Babylon where, in June 323 BCE, Alexander *fell ill and died*, possibly by poisoning. **Alexander's son** was not born until after his death, so the empire was shared between his **GENERALS**.

How it changed the world

Alexander's conquests spread Greek culture, language, and ideas across Asia as far as India. He destroyed the Persian empire, and the cities he established (many called Alexandria) strengthened trade between Europe and Asia.

General **SELEUCUS I NICATOR** *ruled over Babylonia. The Seleucid empire he established lasted until 64 BCE. At its height, it spread as far as Afghanistan and northwestern India.*

Alexander's bodyguard, Lysimachus, took over Asia Minor, including the city of Pergamon, which soon fell to his backstabbing lieutenant, **PHILETAERUS** *(left). He founded the Attalid dynasty, which ruled Asia Minor till 133 BCE.*

Teotihuacan comes of age

Mesoamerican METROPOLIS

Around 450 CE, the city of Teotihuacan – "the birthplace of the gods" – in modern-day Mexico had become one of the largest ancient cities of the Americas.

The Pyramid of the Sun is one of the world's highest pyramids at 75 m (246 ft).

By the way…
I, Mighty Spearthrower Owl, will rule this city for more than 60 years – but I'll never tire of making sacrifices to the gods.

Multicultural mix

The city's origins are **shrouded in mystery**, but building probably began about 100 BCE. At its peak, Teotihuacan was home to as many as 125,000 people. It traded with other **central American** city-states, and even took one over. King Spearthrower Owl, who had roots in the city, conquered the Mayan city of **TIKAL**, and installed one of his sons as king there.

Kings were religious leaders as well as rulers.

What came before...

The **TOTONAC** of eastern Mexico claimed they built Teotihuacan. Totonacs certainly lived in the city, but there's no evidence they built it.

To build on the swampy land, the Teotihuacanos created chinampas (reed islands) crisscrossed by canals. These chinampas at **XOCHIMILCO** date to Aztec times.

City slickers

There was no jumble of streets in Teotihuacan's city centre. It was built on a **neat grid** with a wide avenue lined with pyramid platforms for making sacrifices. The landmark **PYRAMIDS** of the Sun and Moon stood to the north of the avenue, and the **Temple of Quetzalcoatl** was to the south. The ceremonial zone made up only a tenth of the city – there were also built-up suburbs packed with housing complexes.

The Avenue of the Dead was so called as it looks like there are tombs on either side.

This mural from a Teotihuacano palace shows a priest in a feathered headdress.

Religion, ritual, and art

Teotihuacanos worshipped many **GODS**. Priests kept the gods happy with animal and **human sacrifices**. Besides painting spectacular murals, the people of Teotihuacan also made **striking pottery**, jewellery, and masks.

How it changed the world

Teotihuacano culture spread to the Maya, Aztecs, and others. Those peoples worshipped similar gods and copied Teotihuacan's style of architecture. The Aztecs even used the same method of building on floating reed islands.

What came after...

The city's end is as much a mystery as its beginning. In the 600s, TEOTIHUACAN was abandoned and buildings were burned. Perhaps there was a revolt?

The AZTECS used to make pilgrimages to the ruins of Teotihuacan. They believed it was the birthplace of the Sun god, Tonatiuh, shown here on their calendar stone.

Coronation of Charlemagne

The FATHER of European unity

In 800 CE, Charles the Great (better known as Charlemagne) was crowned emperor in Rome. He was the first emperor in the West for more than 300 years.

Charlemagne had co-ruled with his brother Carloman for three years – until his brother mysteriously died!

Ruler on the rampage

Charlemagne had become sole ruler of the **Franks** in 771 CE, and was on a mission to *dominate Europe*. By 774, he was king of Italy. Over the next 30 years he advanced into Spain, captured Bavaria, defeated the Avars near Belgrade, and **SMASHED THE SAXONS** of northern Germany.

Did you know? Charlemagne was part of the Carolingian dynasty (descendants of the military leader Charles Martel).

Seat of power

Charlemagne made **Aachen** (in the far west of modern-day Germany) his power base and capital. He built a *palace and cathedral* there. The only part of the palace still standing is the **PALATINE CHAPEL** (left), which contains Charlemagne's tomb.

What came before...

CLOVIS I *was the first king to unite the Franks. He converted to Christianity in 496 CE and had reconquered much of Roman Gaul by his death in 511.*

Charlemagne encouraged good relations with the Church, and protected **POPE LEO III** *from his enemies. In return, Leo lent religious support to Charlemagne.*

Emperor of the Romans

In 800 CE, Charlemagne was ruler of most of western Europe. On **Christmas Day** that year, Pope Leo III crowned him **EMPEROR OF THE ROMANS**. The coronation enraged Byzantine Empress Irene in Constantinople, but she could do nothing to stop it. Charlemagne was officially the *"Father of Europe"*.

Here, the monk Rabanus Maurus (left) and Alcuin (middle) are presenting their work to Archbishop Odgar of Mainz.

The Carolingian Renaissance

Charlemagne could not read, but he knew the *power of education*. He surrounded himself with top scholars, such as the historian Alcuin of York. **Monastic schools** grew up across the empire, where monks hand-copied precious **LATIN MANUSCRIPTS**. Under Charlemagne, art, literature, music, and learning all flourished.

> **By the way...**
> My military campaigns doubled the size of the Frankish Kingdom!

How it changed the world

Charlemagne united most of what would eventually become France, and the eastern part of his empire later formed the core of the future Germany. His promotion of learning and education helped to show how a leader could improve the lives of his subjects.

What came after...

Charlemagne wanted a standard script used in books across his empire. The resulting **CAROLINGIAN MINISCULE** *was the basis of our lower-case alphabet.*

Many of Charlemagne's descendants, and later powerful rulers, were crowned "Emperor of the Romans" or "Holy Roman Emperor". **OTTO THE GREAT** *was the first in 962.*

Dreadful disasters

The FATEFUL events
that happened at random

Sometimes Mother Nature or human error throws up completely unexpected events that change everything. Though shocking, often much can be learned from these one-off incidents.

This man was cowering as he tried to avoid the toxic fumes of Mount Vesuvius's eruption.

Spanish Armada destroyed

England *was in deep trouble* when the greatest naval fleet in the world, the Spanish **ARMADA**, engaged England in battle in 1588. But, through some clever tactics, aided by their smaller and more manoeuvrable ships, the English managed to scatter the Armada. Before the Armada could regroup, it sailed right into a massive storm that **wrecked as many as a third of its ships**, handing victory to the English.

By the way...
The Armada was sent by Spain to stop Protestantism and overthrow Queen Elizabeth I of England.

Mount Vesuvius erupts

When the volcano Mount Vesuvius erupted in 79 CE, it buried the Roman city of **POMPEII** that lay nearby, but the ash and molten rock strangely preserved the city too. After excavation in 1798 onwards, the town was able to tell its story again. Whole streets, houses, people, and even pieces of art were uncovered, **perfectly preserved** in the rock, meaning Pompeii's terrible disaster helped us to better *understand the Roman world*.

The *Titanic* sinks

Though the RMS *Titanic* was dubbed "the unsinkable ship", the **largest ocean liner** of its time hit an iceberg and sank in the Atlantic Ocean just four days into its first voyage. *More than 1,500 people died* in the disaster, but the lessons learned led to improved safety: ships started carrying enough **LIFEBOATS** for all passengers, and installed equipment to help communicate better with other ships.

⇧ Only 706 people survived the Titanic

The Bhola Cyclone

The *deadliest tropical cyclone* ever recorded claimed up to 500,000 lives in Bhola, East Pakistan, in 1970. The Pakistan government's relief effort was heavily criticized, and soon **fighting** spread throughout the province. After nearly nine months of battling, during which India fought alongside the rebels, Pakistan was defeated and its former province became the independent state of **BANGLADESH**.

A tidal wave accompanied the cyclone's 185 Kp/h (115 mph) winds that devastated the coast.

Chernobyl nuclear explosion

Nuclear power plants use the **energy stored inside atoms** to generate power. In the early hours of 26 April 1986, part of the Chernobyl Nuclear Power Plant in Ukraine (then part of the Soviet Union) exploded, ripping the plant apart. **RADIOACTIVE MATERIAL**, causing death and illness, was sent high into the atmosphere, and eventually spread as far as the UK. The disaster increased distrust within the Soviet Union of the state authorities, who sought to *conceal the explosion*.

The Silk Road starts

The superhighway to the EXOTIC East

By the way…
During my 54-year rule, I expanded China's borders in all directions.

Travelled by merchants, monks, and explorers, the Silk Road was a series of interconnecting routes that stretched from the riches of China 6,500 km (4,000 miles) overland to Europe.

The secret of silk

The first evidence of **silk production** in China dates to 2500 BCE, but according to legend, **EMPRESS LEIZU** (wife of Huangdi) introduced the silkworm as early as 3000 BCE. This talented queen invented the loom, too. Silkmaking was a closely guarded state secret – revealing any detail outside China was *punishable by death*!

Han power

East-West trade developed during the *Han Dynasty* (206 BCE to 220 CE). To boost it, the seventh Han emperor, **WU**, sent envoys carrying silks to Persia and Mesopotamia. Han officials **controlled the Silk Road** as far as central Asia. Beyond that, the Persians ruled, and from 30 BCE the western end was in the Roman empire.

What came before...

The SCYTHIANS *were among the first long-distance traders in the region. They had links with China, India, Persia, and Greece from the 800s BCE.*

In the 400s BCE, Darius I of Persia built a 2,500-km (1,550-mile) ROYAL ROAD. *It connected Sardis (in what is now Turkey) and Susa (in what is now Iran).*

Silkworm eggs

Stolen silk

A lot of China's raw **SILK** ended up in the Byzantine empire, where skilled textile workers turned it into fine, colourful fabrics to sell across Europe. That was not enough for Emperor **Justinian**. In the 500s CE, he paid two monks to *smuggle silkworm eggs* out of China. At last Byzantium could make its own silk. China's monopoly was over.

How it changed the world

Travellers didn't just carry silk along the Silk Road. It also opened up trade of all sorts, and the exchange of ideas, religions, and diseases!

Emperor Wu grew rich through trade along the Silk Road.

West meets East

The Italian explorer *Marco Polo* travelled along the Silk Road in the 1270s. He reached the court of the Mongol emperor, **Kublai Khan**. His account of his **ADVENTURES** in the exotic East fascinated European readers.

What came after...

In 1453, Constantinople fell to the Ottoman sultan, **MEHMED II**. The Turks now controlled land trade with the East. Europeans looked for alternatives to the Silk Road.

During the 1400s and 1500s, **EUROPEAN EXPLORERS** discovered new sea routes to India and China. Silks and spices reached Europe on boats, not camel caravans.

Fall of Constantinople

In 1453, OTTOMAN ruler Mehmed II put an end to the Byzantine empire

Rise of the Turks

The **Ottoman empire** began in modern-day Turkey in the 1300s. The Ottomans were soon sweeping across the Middle East, and into Europe until all that was left of the Byzantine empire (also known as the eastern Roman empire) was a small area around the capital, **CONSTANTINOPLE**. The city's walls had never been breached, but the Ottomans used heavy artillery to **smash them down**. After a two-month siege, Ottoman sultan Mehmed II walked into a devastated city.

Constantine XI was killed during the siege.

End of an era

The fall of the city **drastically changed Europe**. In one swoop, the Muslim Ottomans had seized the centre of the Orthodox Christian religion, effectively closed the trade routes between Asia and Europe, and, in deposing Byzantine Emperor **CONSTANTINE XI** (left), ended the last surviving part of the Roman empire. Constantinople became known as "Istanbul", and became the **capital of the Ottoman empire** until it fell in 1922.

How it changed...
Aside from ending the Roman empire, Constantinople's fall forced Europeans to look West to get to the East.

the world

The painting caption:
Ivan struck his son with his sceptre.

A "terrible" family murder

In 1581, Russian Tsar Ivan IV (also known as *Ivan the Terrible*) killed his son and heir in a fit of rage. This placed his youngest, rather sickly, son **FEODOR** next in line to the throne. Feodor had no interest in running Russia, but when his father died in 1584, he had no choice. He was a weak leader and left the business of ruling to his wife's brother, a boyar (Russian prince) called **Boris Godunov**.

In all, there were two more False Dmitris after the first one.

False Dmitri

When Tsar Feodor died in 1598 without an heir, Godunov seized the throne, and Russia's **Time of Troubles** began. A terrible famine from 1601–1603 killed a third of the population. In 1603, Polish forces entered Russia, supporting **FALSE DMITRI**'s claim to the throne. He said he was Feodor's half-brother Dmitri (who had actually died in 1591). When Godunov died in 1605, False Dmitri was made tsar – but he was *murdered a year later*.

By the way…
I burst into tears when I was asked to be tsar! But I was smiling by the time I was crowned in February 1613.

The Time of Troubles

15 years of chaos in Russia before young Mikhail ROMANOV becomes tsar

Romanov Russia

A Russian prince called **Vasily Shuisky** tried his hand at being tsar next, but he was replaced by the Polish king, *Wladyslaw IV Vasa,* in 1610. Determined to drive out the Poles, Russian forces finally tasted victory in August 1612. Russia's nobles elected a distant 16-year-old relative of Ivan the Terrible, **MIKHAIL ROMANOV** (left) to be tsar.

How it changed…

The Romanovs reigned for 300 years. The Time of Troubles led to the most stable period in Russia's history.

the world

87

Columbus reaches the Americas

How the Americas came to be colonized by Europe

In 1492, Italian sailor Christopher Columbus sailed west across the Atlantic hoping to reach India. Instead he found the Americas – by accident! He was the first European to land there for almost 500 years.

West to India

Christopher Columbus thought he could find a *sea route* to Asia by sailing west. Since Constantinople had fallen to the Ottoman empire in 1453, the land route to Asia involved passing through hostile Muslim territory. **Ferdinand and Isabella of Spain**, who had recently kicked the **MUSLIMS** out of their country, agreed to fund Columbus.

Columbus's first voyage

Columbus set off in summer 1492 with three ships, the **SANTA MARIA**, *Pinta*, and *Niña*, and 90 men. After five long weeks at sea, a lookout on the *Pinta* sighted land. They anchored on an island in the **Bahamas**, inhabited by the Arawak people. Columbus claimed the land for Spain, and established a colony on *Hispaniola* (modern-day Haiti).

What came before...

In 1002, Viking explorer **LEIF ERICSSON** *sailed west from Greenland and reached what was probably Newfoundland, Canada. He founded a colony called Vinland.*

In 1498, Portuguese explorer **VASCO DA GAMA** *became the first European to reach India by sea. His route took him around Africa to the Indian Ocean.*

Uneasy legacy

Columbus made **three further expeditions** in 1493, 1498, and 1502. For a long time, Europeans saw him as a hero, but he brought suffering to **NATIVE** populations. His reputation was not spotless with colonists, either. In 1500, settlers on Hispaniola sent Columbus **back to Spain in chains**, accusing him of brutality to the local people.

Columbus named the place he landed "San Salvador".

By the way...
I kept two log books – one for myself and one for the mutinous crew (in which I lied about how far we'd travelled)!

The Arawaks were friendly and traded with the crew.

Did you know?
Columbus called the first people he met "Indians" because he thought he was in India.

How it changed the world

Columbus's discovery opened up the Americas for colonization. The "New World" was a source of gold, silver, tobacco, and new foods. In turn, Europeans introduced technologies and religion, but also brought slaves and disease.

What came after...

On his voyages to South America (1499–1502), Italian **AMERIGO VESPUCCI** showed that the "New World" was not Asia after all. The Americas are named after him.

In 1519, **FERDINAND MAGELLAN** of Portugal set out to sail around the world, entering the Pacific from the Atlantic. He died on the way, but 18 crew completed the voyage.

Exciting explorations

Pushing into NEW LANDS and making exciting discoveries

Various globetrotters have blazed a trail over the years. By exploring new lands and encountering foreign cultures, these explorers have also added to human knowledge, and helped spread and exchange ideas.

Ibn Battuta wrote about his travels in a book called the *Rihla*.

Ibn Battuta

In 1325, Ibn Battuta set off from his native Morocco on a hajj (Muslim pilgrimage) to the holy city of **MECCA** (in modern-day Saudi Arabia). Bitten by the travelling bug, he stayed on the road for *nearly 30 years*. His adventures took him to India, China, and all over the Muslim world, including to the famed city of **Timbuktu**. Ibn Battuta also picked up at least eight wives along the way!

Zheng He may have visited up to 30 countries.

Admiral Zheng He

Between 1405 and 1433, the Chinese admiral Zheng He led *seven expeditions* to southern and western Asia and east Africa, on behalf of three different **MING** emperors. His huge fleet was made up of more than 300 ships. Along the way, Zheng He gave gifts of Chinese silk, gold, and porcelain. He returned with foreign riches for the emperor, including a pet **giraffe**.

Captain James Cook

In 1768, the British government sent navigator James Cook to **explore the Pacific Ocean** to see if there was any land there. Aboard his ship the *Endeavour*, Cook found and mapped the coasts of Hawaii, eastern Australia, and New Zealand. He landed at Stingray Bay (later renamed **Botany Bay**) and claimed **AUSTRALIA** for Britain. On his second voyage (1772), Cook became the first person to cross the Antarctic Circle.

Farmer's son Cook joined the merchant navy aged 17, and the Royal Navy aged 27.

Did you know?
Cook was killed on his third voyage, after a dispute with the natives of Hawaii.

A Shoshoni woman called Sacajawea guided Lewis and Clark.

Lewis and Clark

In 1804, Meriwether Lewis and William Clark captained an expedition into the uncharted **AMERICAN WEST**. President Jefferson had asked them to explore the **Louisiana Territory** that he had bought the previous year. It took Lewis and Clark 18 months to cross the Rocky Mountains along the **Oregon Trail** and reach the Pacific coast.

Roald Amundsen

Norwegian explorer Roald Amundsen arrived at the **South Pole** on 14 December 1911, after a race to the bottom of the Earth against British naval officer **Robert Scott**. Amundsen's expedition was carefully planned and well equipped, using skis and **DOG SLEDS** for transportation. Scott and his men did make it to the pole (a month after the Norwegians), but they all died on the return journey. The Amundsen-Scott South Pole research station is named after these courageous explorers.

Amundsen wore Inuit-style furs to keep out the cold and the wet.

Tasman's voyages

A Dutch seafarer maps a whole NEW CONTINENT

In two voyages of 1642 and 1644, Abel Tasman reached Tasmania and New Zealand and mapped the northern coast of Australia.

The southern continent

The Greek thinker Aristotle was the first to say that there must be a **Terra Australis** (south land) to balance out the continents in the northern hemisphere. The imaginary continent was drawn on **MAPS** long before Dutch sailor Willem Janszoon became the first recorded European to set foot in Australia in 1606. Surprisingly, **Aristotle was right**!

TYPVS ORBIS TERRARVM

This world map from the 1500s shows the huge *Terra Australis* running along the bottom.

The Dutch East India Company built warehouses and shipyards in Amsterdam.

Trading superpower

The **Dutch East India Company** was set up in 1602 so Dutch merchants could dominate European **trade with Asia**, especially the money-making buying and selling of **SPICES**. Its employees built ships and forts, and explored possible new markets around the globe.

What came before...

Australia's first peoples, the Aboriginal Australians, reached the southern continent about 50,000 years ago. The **MAORI** arrived in New Zealand about 1250. They were hostile towards early European explorers.

Tasman's first voyage

Dutch seafarer **Abel Tasman** joined the Dutch East India Company in 1633. In 1642, the company sent him to explore "Beach", a mysterious place on maps that was thought to be part of the *Terra Australis*. Tasman sighted Tasmania on 24 November. He named it ***Van Diemen's Land*** after the Governor-General of the Dutch East Indies (modern-day Indonesia). Then winds blew him off course to New Zealand, where Maori warriors in canoes **ATTACKED ONE OF HIS BOATS**.

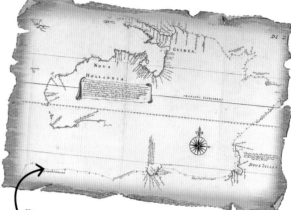

Tasman commanded two ships on his first voyage: the Heemskerck and the Zeehaen.

Tasman's map of New Holland (Australia)

Map man

In **1644**, Tasman set out again. He **mapped** the north coast of what he called New Holland (Australia). The east coast remained largely unknown for more than a century, when British explorer James Cook **CLAIMED THE CONTINENT** for Britain in 1770.

How it changed... the world

Tasman paved the way for a new continent being opened up to European settlement. Sadly, colonization led to the destruction of the indigenous peoples' ways of life.

What came after...

From 1789, **PRISON SHIPS** carried criminals to Australia from Britain to live out their lives in penal colonies.

AUSTRALIA AND NEW ZEALAND claimed independence from Britain in 1901 and 1907 respectively, but they still have the British Queen as their head of state.

The last tsar

Tsar Nicholas II of Russia **ABDICATED** (stepped down) after the February Revolution of 1917, ending 300 years of Romanov rule. Mounting casualties in **World War I**, combined with mass anger at his blocking of democratic reforms, forced him from power, leading to *a people's government*.

Nicholas (middle) and his family were imprisoned after he abdicated.

Lenin whipped up the crowds upon his return.

Lenin returns

A revolutionary turns Russia into a COMMUNIST state

By the way...
As my hero Karl Marx, the father of Communism, said: "The workers have nothing to lose... but their chains!"

Bolshevik troops storm the Winter Palace, where the tsar used to live.

The October Revolution

In October 1917, Lenin told his political party, the **BOLSHEVIKS**, it was time to revolt. The weak government gave **little resistance** as Bolshevik troops seized key government buildings. Lenin took Russia out of the war, and declared Russia a workers' republic, which, along with other parts of the former Tsarist empire, became the *Union of Soviet Socialist Republics* (USSR) in 1922.

Revolutionary returns

Vladimir Lenin had been **banished from Russia** for urging workers to seize and then share power equally, a revolutionary idea that is called **COMMUNISM**. Russia's enemy in the war, Germany, offered him safe passage back to Russia, hoping he would take Russia out of the war. Lenin returned in 1917 to a *country in disarray*.

How it changed...
The USSR became the world's first communist state, and inspired similar revolutions in China, Cuba, Vietnam, and North Korea.
the world

94

Hitler seizes power

A FASCIST becomes German chancellor, leading to another terrible world war

The Nazis often held rallies and other public events in a show of power.

Looking for answers

After World War I, there was **political unrest** in Europe. Some believed communism (power to the workers) was the answer. Others, such as Mussolini in Italy and Hitler in Germany, believed in a form of nationalism called **FASCISM**, where a strong leader controlled society, made up of *people of the same race*, while those of different races were persecuted.

Mussolini became an ally of Hitler's.

The Nazis

Hitler became leader of the fascist **NAZI** (national socialist) party in 1921. When the *German economy collapsed* in 1927, the Nazi Party began to gain seats in the Reichstag (German parliament). Hitler's speeches blamed the Jews and other minorities for Germany's problems, and promised to **make the country strong again**.

Total power

In January 1933, Hitler became **CHANCELLOR** (leader) and formed a government. In March, he took advantage of an arson attack on the **Reichstag** (left) to cement his iron rule. By August 1934, he was *dictator of Germany*, and his destructive reign would change the world for ever.

How it changed...
As dictator, Hitler began to kill the Nazi Party's enemies. His attempt to expand Germany's borders led to World War II, in which millions died.
the world

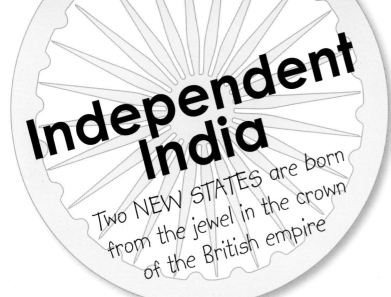

Independent India

Two NEW STATES are born from the jewel in the crown of the British empire

On 15 August 1947, Jawaharlal Nehru became prime minister of the newly independent India, a country that had been under British control for nearly 200 years.

By the way...
At last! I've been calling for Indian independence for 30 years!

Nehru had been head of the Indian government before independence.

Peaceful protest

From the 1920s, **Mahatma Gandhi** (left) led the movement for Indian independence. He encouraged *peaceful protest*, such as marching against British laws, or **REFUSING TO OBEY** them altogether. Gandhi's non-violent approach began to work, but cracks started to appear among the Hindu, Sikh, and Muslim religious groups.

One state or two?

Britain promised to hand over power after World War II. Indian Hindus, including Gandhi, wanted one single state, but **MUSLIMS**, led by **Muhammad Ali Jinnah**, wanted their own separate state. The Brits agreed, after a *Direct Action Day* of Muslim protests ended in thousands of deaths.

Jinnah disagreed with Gandhi over many things, including non-violent protest.

What came before...

From 1757 to 1858, Britain's East India Company took control of India, driving out rival Portuguese and Dutch traders. Some states, such as the **Tipu Sultan**'s Mysore, put up fierce resistance.

In 1857, the Indians rebelled when a rifle issued to Indians in the army offended Hindus and Muslims. The British government took direct control and the **Raj** (empire) had begun.

Partition and independence

Lord Louis Mountbatten, Britain's top representative in India, was in charge of India's **PARTITION** (splitting in two). On 14 August 1947, he handed over a Muslim homeland made up of regions in the northwest and northeast of India, called **Pakistan**, to Jinnah, its new leader. The next day, the area left became the independent state of *India*, with Nehru as its leader.

Millions on the move

The partitioning led to the *greatest mass-migration* of people in history. About 7 million Hindus and Sikhs fled Pakistan for India, while about the same number of Muslims went the other way. They went **on foot, in carts, and on trains**. A million people lost their lives in **RIOTS**, while many others died from hunger, thirst, or exhaustion.

Lord Mountbatten had fought for Britain in World War II.

Ordinary people on both sides gave up their homes to escape potential religious oppression.

How it changed the world

India is now the world's second-largest country by population, with a fast-growing economy. It is also the world's largest democracy. The relationship between India and Pakistan has been very tense, with occasional outbreaks of fighting.

What came after...

Kashmir had the choice of joining India or Pakistan. Its Hindu ruler, **MAHARAJAH HARI SINGH**, chose India, but its people were mostly Muslim. India and Pakistan warred over Kashmir in 1947–1948 and again in 1965.

West and East Pakistan were 1,700 km (870 miles) apart. In 1971, civil war broke out between the two. After the war ended, East Pakistan became a new, separate country, **BANGLADESH**.

The Long March

A 12-month trek across China that cemented Mao's route to power

Nationalist leader Chiang Kai-Shek fought against the Qing dynasty in 1911.

Early defeat

In October 1934, China's ruling Nationalist Party, led by Chiang Kai-Shek, blockaded the revolutionary communist Red Army in the southeast of the country, led by **Mao Zedong**. Though almost eliminated, the Red Army managed to flee through the Nationalist lines, and retreated.

How it changed... the world

Mao's controversial leadership ended with his death in 1976. China is the second-largest economy in the world, and is still led by the Communist Party.

On the move

The retreat, known as the **LONG MARCH**, saw the communists walk more than 9,500 km (6,000 miles) to the north, over some of the country's **most difficult terrain**. Of the 86,000 soldiers who set out, just 8,000 reached the new communist headquarters at Yan'an in October 1935. The march brought the army closer together, and helped Mao **shape his political ideas**.

Communist China

Japan occupied China from 1937 to 1945, retreating after World War II. Mao stepped up his **attacks** against the Nationalists. In January 1949, with clever military tactics, the Red Army captured China's capital, **BEIJING**, and established the **People's Republic of China**. Mao's wait was over, but it was just the beginning for communism's uneasy history in China.

Mao's followers founded communes for farm workers, shown here in a propaganda poster.

This passport of a German Jew allowed the holder to settle in Palestine.

The birth of Israel
How the JEWISH state came to be

Palestine

After World War I, the Middle Eastern state of Palestine was ruled by Britain. Its mostly **Muslim Arab population** was unhappy about Jewish settlers called **ZIONISTS** who were calling for a Jewish state to be carved out of Palestine. There was *violence on both sides*.

The promised land

In 1947, a plan emerged to split Palestine into Jewish and Arab states with Jerusalem under international administration. Instead, civil war broke out and on *14 May 1948*, **David Ben-Gurion** became the first prime minister of the newly created Jewish state, **ISRAEL**.

Polish-born David Ben-Gurion had been a key figure in the Zionist movement.

Israeli soldiers attack during the Arab-Israeli War.

Jerusalem is a holy city for Jews, Muslims, and Christians.

How it changed...

Israel provided a home for the world's Jews, but the birth of the state has caused big problems with its Muslim neighbours.

...the world

Troubled times

Muslim states refused to recognize Israel, and a series of **CONFLICTS** followed, starting with the *Arab-Israeli War* of 1948–1949. Against all the odds, Israel managed to survive **and even prosper** in this time.

achievements

Some of the greatest moments in human history have come from people chasing interesting and beautiful ideas until they produce something amazing. From scientific breakthroughs to wonderful pieces of art, to breathtaking buildings and new ways to read – the advances in this chapter have all helped us to explain and enjoy the world, and to bring us all closer together.

Reckless records

Before writing came about, people had no way to easily keep track of the things they owned and made. **FARMERS**, for example, would rely on sight alone to make decisions on how much produce they had harvested, and how much they could sell – *but the eyes can deceive!*

Cuneiform script, from modern-day Iraq, is one of the earliest examples of writing.

This cuneiform tablet records food and drink.

Getting symbolic

Traders often used **stones** to represent the things they owned. Around 4000 BCE, some bright spark began to use **SYMBOLS** inscribed in clay instead. One of the earliest examples we have comes from the Sumerian culture in Ur (modern-day Iraq). These became more sophisticated, and proper *writing had begun* by 3200 BCE.

First writing

How we SCRATCHED and SCRAPED our very first words

How it changed...

Writing allows us to communicate with each other, but also to preserve information for future generations.

the world

"Hieroglyph" means "sacred carving" in Greek

This hieroglyph of a fat bird was the symbol used for the sound "S".

Sounds like...

The process was complete a little later on when symbols known as **HIEROGLYPHS** came into fashion. These represented sounds – making the written symbol a representative of **how to pronounce** the word for the first time. Today, *our symbols are letters*, but the idea is the same.

Loosening up

Before farmers plant crops, they plough (loosen) the soil, but doing it by hand or with a shovel is *hard and time-consuming*. In the 6th century BCE, farmers developed the **ARD** – an early kind of wooden plough that broke the ground as it was dragged behind an animal.

The ard was first used in what is now Iraq and Pakistan.

The ardhead dug up the soil in a straight line, allowing seeds to be sown in the path left behind.

Wheely useful

As the idea *tore the soil* around the world, other people improved it. The Romans added a **WHEEL,** making the plough much easier to move and control, and they made the ploughshares (the part that dug into the soil) out of **iron**, which was very strong and cut into the ground more easily.

Adding more ploughshares reduced ploughing time even more.

The plough

The FARMING revolution that allowed more food to be produced in a fraction of the time

How it changed...

The plough was the first tool to improve food production by taking a lot of the time and effort out of sowing crops.

the world

Modern times

Though the **plough** has been *improved and refined* since ancient times, it still works in the same way. Modern ploughs are made of metal and pulled by **TRACTORS**.

Discovery of bronze

How METALS made life easier

The birth of bronze

By 3250 BCE, people had learned how to **EXTRACT METALS FROM ROCKS** by heating them. Then they found that mixing a soft, red metal called **copper with a little tin** made a new metal that was tough, but still easy to shape. This *useful new stuff was called bronze*.

When people worked out how to mix metals to make bronze, they soon realized it was the perfect material for all kinds of tools and weapons.

Items were cast in moulds or hammered from flat sheets of bronze.

Sticks and stones

Palaeolithic, or **Stone-Age, people** could use only **WOOD OR STONE** to make the tools they needed. But wood snapped easily and rotted quickly, and stone was difficult to shape, so early *tools and weapons were rather basic*.

What came before...

The first metals that humans learned to use were GOLD AND SILVER. *Both metals could be found naturally in the ground and were soft enough to be shaped without heating.*

The COPPER AGE *began around 6500 BCE, in the Middle East. Copper was slightly harder than gold and silver, so could be used to make tools or weapons.*

Melting and moulding

Bronze was made by casting – heating copper and tin until they were liquid, then **pouring into moulds** and allowing to cool and set. **BRONZE FARMING TOOLS** made it easier to clear forests for planting crops so, for the first time, people could *grow enough food to sell*, not just to feed their families.

Objects could be cast in many different shapes to suit the job they were designed for.

Bronze-Age Britons lived together in wooden roundhouses, thatched with reeds or straw.

By the way...
The oldest toy ever found in Europe is a bronze figure of a stork, thought to be 3,500 years old.

All over the world

By 2000 BCE, the **BRONZE AGE** had arrived in Europe from its beginnings in the Middle East, and **developed separately** in Asia and the Americas. Farms grew bigger, and more and more *people settled in communities*, which became villages and towns.

How it changed the world

Bronze led to big changes in the way people earned a living. With better tools, people could farm the land for profit. Miners and craftspeople appeared – and traders, who bought and sold both metal and finished goods.

What came after...

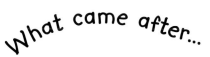

THE IRON AGE *was the next leap forward in technology. Iron was more common than copper and tin, and it made tools that were stronger and longer-lasting than bronze.*

In the 19th century, people discovered a cheap way to **MASS-PRODUCE STEEL**. *Strong and flexible, steel is ideal for large structures such as bridges.*

Building the Great Wall
Old, strong, and very LONG!

Built to keep invaders out, China's Great Wall is the world's longest man-made structure.

Carriageway

Signal beacon

About a million soldiers guarded the wall from watchtowers like this.

Emperor Qin Shi Huang
The **PLAN FOR THE GREAT WALL** was hatched in 221 BCE by the first emperor of China, **Qin Shi Huang**. A fearsome warrior, he became *ruler of Qin state*, then conquered the six other Chinese states and united them into one nation.

What came before...

The magnificent walls of the ancient CITY OF BABYLON, built around 575 BCE, were reported to be so wide that chariot races were held on them.

The LONG WALLS of Athens were built to protect the city from sieges. They were destroyed in 405 BCE when the Spartans defeated the Athenian fleet, and demanded the walls be torn down (shown here).

Did you know?
Hundreds of beacon towers along the Wall's length allowed soldiers guarding the Wall to send messages to each other.

Keep out!

Emperor Qin ordered that all the walls on China's northern border be connected, creating a **CONTINUOUS WALL** to keep out foreign raiders. Later emperors added sections to make the wall even longer. By the 16th century, it stretched for a *mind-boggling 8,850 km* (5,500 miles).

Hard labour

Up to **a million workers** helped to build the wall – mainly soldiers, prisoners, and peasants who were **FORCED TO WORK** on the project. Made from *stone, earth, sticks, and bricks*, the wall is up to 9 m (30 ft) thick and 7.5 m (25 ft) high.

Ramparts

Bamboo scaffolding

Bricks were held together with a mortar of lime mixed with glutinous rice.

How it changed the world

The wall helped the Chinese people feel safe. Free from the costs and worry of war, China became the world's richest, most powerful empire.

Large, locally quarried rocks

What came after...

In the 15th century, Emperor Yong Lo built THE FORBIDDEN CITY *in Beijing. It was an enormous palace complex, with more than 8,700 rooms.*

China was ruled by emperors for more than 2,000 years. The last emperor was PUYI, *who was overthrown in 1912 when China became a republic.*

Building beauties

Lessons from the past about building to IMPRESS

Solid history in brick and stone, these famous ancient buildings have inspired artists, architects, and engineers for centuries.

The Great Pyramid

Built about 2600 BCE, the Great Pyramid of Giza in Egypt (centre) is the tomb of a *pharaoh* named Khufu. It is made of **2,600,000 STONE BLOCKS** and once stood 137 m (488 ft) tall. For 4,000 years, it **was the tallest building in the world**, until topped by the Eiffel Tower in 1889. The pyramids of Khufu's son and grandson sit on either side of it.

Huge, carved faces look out from Angkor Wat's towers.

Did you know?
Cambodians love Angkor Wat so much that they put it on their national flag.

Angkor Wat

The *12th-century* temple complex of Angkor Wat in Cambodia is the largest religious building in the world. Although much of the original temple has **VANISHED**, the site still covers more than 400 km² (155 sq miles). Originally dedicated to the Hindu god Vishnu, it **became a Buddhist temple** in the 13th century.

Machu Picchu

The builders of this **ANCIENT INCA CITY** near Cuzco in Peru had very primitive tools, but they cut and placed the stones so accurately a knife wouldn't slide between them. The site, *possibly a royal estate*, dates to about 1450. It **spreads across 700 terraces** high in the Andes.

Terraces carved out from the steep mountainside were used for farming.

By the way...
In different lights, the Taj Mahal changes colour, from pink in the morning, to white in the afternoon, and golden in moonlight.

"Taj Mahal" means "crown of palaces".

Taj Mahal

It took about 20,000 workers *more than 20 years* to build the Taj Mahal, and 1,000 elephants to transport the materials. The **WHITE MARBLE TOMB** at Agra, in India, was completed in 1643. It commemorates the Mughal Emperor Shah Jahan's wife, **Mumtaz Mahal**, who died giving birth to her 14th child.

⬇ The mosque's walls are up to 61 cm (24 in) thick

Great Mosque of Djenné

The sun-baked mosque at Djenné, in Mali, West Africa, is the **largest mud-brick building** in the world. An early version, built in 1240, helped Djenné to become one of Africa's *most important Islamic learning centres*. The mosque seen today was built in a year from 1906, to the same plan as the old mosque. It is still a respected **RELIGIOUS MONUMENT**.

109

Ink was applied to the etchings, which printed when pressed to another surface.

Chinese blocks

Avid readers in **CHINA** were enjoying the printed word and image long before anyone else. Chinese printers used *etched wood and clay blocks* from about 600 CE to print images and text onto **paper or cloth**.

Printed words

Allowing WORDS to spread across the world further than ever before

Pressed to impress

Europe got the *printed word* in about 1450. German inventor Johannes Gutenberg developed letters made of **METAL** that could be arranged and rearranged inside a wooden grid. These were covered in ink and pressed hard onto paper, printing a **whole page each time**.

This Bible in Latin from 1455 is one of Gutenberg's first printed books.

Gutenberg's printing press could mass-produce a page in a matter of minutes.

Printing power

By **1500**, printing presses were in operation in most *major cities of Europe*. The availability of printed books made it easier for everyone to learn to read, and for ideas to spread **FAR AND WIDE**, leading to many scientific discoveries in the years ahead.

How it changed...

Printed books brought knowledge and entertainment wherever they went, and meant that everyone could have access to them, too.

the world

Hangul alphabet

An invention that gave Korean people the LETTERS to write their own language

King Sejong's idea

Before the mid-15th century, **KOREANS** wrote their own language in Chinese script. Only a few educated people knew how to do it. Around 1443, the Korean monarch, **King Sejong**, decided this was wrong. He believed that all his subjects should be able to write – and even send him letters of complaint if they wanted to. So he *invented a new alphabet for them*.

This is a sample of Hangul writing. In modern times, just 24 letters are used, as four of the originals have been dropped.

By the way...
It took ages for my alphabet to catch on. The aristocrats never liked it, and then Hangul was banned for a time in the 16th century.

Korean script

King Sejong created a special **28-letter alphabet**, which became known as the *Hangul alphabet, or "Hunmin chong-um"*. It is **SO SIMPLE** that most Korean children master it before they start school, and almost everyone in Korea today reads and writes with the Hangul alphabet.

How it changed...
Hangul has contributed to Korea's high levels of literacy. The alphabet works well with computers and may have improved communications.

the world

The Mona Lisa

An enigmatic smile that lit up the RENAISSANCE

The world's most famous painting is a portrait of a young woman with just a hint of a smile, but it represented a revolution in art.

By the way...
You can go and see my *Mona Lisa* at the Louvre Museum in Paris. But, be ready for crowds – lots of people want a look.

Like smoke

Leonardo da Vinci, the Italian artist, scientist, and all-round genius, finished his great work, the *Mona Lisa*, around 1517. The oil painting took more than 14 years to create, no doubt a result of the "**SFUMATO**" technique Leonardo used, where the colours carefully blend in to each other almost like smoke. The painting was so important to him that in the last years of his life he **took it everywhere he went**.

What came before...

The **RENAISSANCE** in arts and learning was made possible by the money of rich patrons like **LORENZO DE MEDICI** *(left) and his family, who were rich bankers in the city of Florence.*

The striking dome of Florence Cathedral, designed by architect **FILIPPO BRUNELLESCHI**, was one of the wonders of the early Renaissance. It was completed in 1436.

Mysterious Mona

For nearly 500 years, the identity of the lady in the painting was a mystery. Then experts discovered in 2005 that the iconic Mona – which means "*young lady*" or "ma'am" – was almost certainly **Lisa Gherardini**, the wife of the rich Florentine silk merchant Francesco del Giocondo. In Italian and French the painting is called "La Gioconda", which is a play on Lisa's husband's name, but also means "**HAPPY**" or "jovial".

Before they knew who Mona Lisa really was, some people said Leonardo modelled the woman on himself!

The famous smile

Mona Lisa's strange little smile **intrigues viewers**. Is she happy or not? Look directly at her eyes, and at the edges of your gaze you'll catch a glimpse of a smile. Look at her lips and the **SMILE HAS GONE**. This is due to the way the eye picks up or blurs details according to its centre of focus. It is thought that Leonardo **deliberately created** this effect.

The ceiling of the Sistine Chapel in the Vatican was painted by Renaissance artist Michelangelo.

How it changed the world

With his "sfumato" method, Leonardo introduced artists to a revolutionary way of working. In creating one of the most-viewed paintings in the world, he has also helped millions of people to appreciate art.

The Renaissance

The Mona Lisa was created during the Renaissance (meaning "rebirth"), the world's **most important artistic period**, which lasted about 200 years from 1350. Renaissance painters, sculptors, architects, and writers took the **best ideas from the past** and looked at them in **NEW WAYS**. The resulting explosion of masterpieces still astonishes us today.

The Renaissance reached northern Europe by the late 15th century. Great works included the "Arnolfini wedding" portrait by Flemish painter **JAN VAN EYCK**.

The High Renaissance of the 1480s saw the best in Italian art. **MICHELANGELO**, *with masterworks like his* **Pietà** *(left), was one of the sculptors and artists who stunned the world.*

Man of many talents

Italian scientist **GALILEO GALILEI** (1564–1642) was brilliant in many ways. His father wanted him to study medicine, but he became a **maths professor** instead, and also taught physics. He was fascinated by astronomy. When a simple telescope, called a spyglass, was invented in 1608, he challenged himself to build a better one that would let him **scan the heavens**.

In Galileo's time, most people didn't understand that the Sun is the centre of the Solar System.

The four moons of Jupiter that Galileo saw are now called the Galilean moons.

The rings of Saturn were seen for the first time by Galileo.

By the way...
I was one of the few scientists who believed the Sun, not Earth, was the centre of the Solar System. This got me into trouble with the Church.

Galileo has been called the "Father of Modern Science".

Looking into space

By 1609, Galileo had **designed and built a telescope** that could magnify things many times more than any previous instrument. It was powerful enough to reveal unimagined astronomical details, such as the **MOUNTAINS OF THE MOON** and the four largest of the moons orbiting the planet Jupiter. Galileo *even saw the rings of Saturn* through his telescope, although he didn't have a clue as to what these might be.

Galileo's telescope

The telescope that allowed us to peer into SPACE

How it changed...
Galileo's invention led to the modern telescopes that have allowed us to learn so much about our place in space.
the world

Mathematical wizard

The English scientist Sir Isaac Newton (1643–1727) used a lot of **BRAINY MATHS** to explain how the world worked. Among other things, he developed the *theory of gravity* and was the first person to explain exactly **what makes objects move**. Newton's ideas, known as his "laws", are still taught to students today.

How it changed...

When Newton worked out scientific laws explaining how the Universe operated, he paved the way for wonders such as space travel.

the world

Newton wrote a very famous book, called *The Principles of Natural Philosophy.*

PHILOSOPHIÆ
NATURALIS
PRINCIPIA
MATHEMATICA.

AUCTORE
ISAACO NEWTONO, Eq. Aur.

Editio tertia aucta & emendata.

LONDINI.

A falling apple may have inspired Newton's thoughts on gravity.

Reaction
Action

⬆ Newton's mother wanted him to be a farmer!

The three laws

Newton's **laws of motion** explain how forces move objects and affect their direction, speed, and distance travelled. The **THIRD LAW** says that for *each action there is a reaction*. For example, if an object is pushed upwards it will exert an equal push downwards.

Newton's laws of motion

Mathematical discoveries that form the basis of modern SCIENCE

Animal antics

These animals have made HEADLINES as heroes, villains, and victims

Animals have often played big roles in the course of history. They've changed the outcome of battles, and made huge scientific advances possible. Here are some who have left their (paw) prints on history!

Did you know?
In both World Wars, homing pigeons were used to carry vital messages from battle fronts, saving hundreds of lives.

Death by tortoise

Writing tragedies was the speciality of the ancient Greek **AESCHYLUS**, but he couldn't have imagined his own **tragic end**. According to legend, he was killed in 456 BCE when an eagle **dropped a tortoise on his bald head**, mistaking it for a rock that would crack the tortoise's shell.

According to legend, Aeschylus was staying outside to avoid a prophecy that he would be killed by a falling object!

The geese were dedicated to the god Juno, and so were deemed sacred.

Guardian geese

In 390 BCE, **Rome was besieged** by the Gauls, who trapped the city's defenders in a fort. One night, the Gauls climbed the fort's walls. The Romans and their guard dogs snored on, but the city's sacred **GEESE WENT MAD**, honking and flapping their wings. Alerted by the hullabaloo, the Romans woke and defeated the Gauls, later **building a temple** to the geese in gratitude.

When Bucephalus died, Alexander founded the city of Bucephala in his honour.

War horse

No one could get the better of a **wild horse** given to Philip II, king of Greece, in 343 BCE. Philip's son, Alexander the Great, saw that the animal was **scared of its own shadow**, and tamed him by taking the bridle and turning the horse's head towards the sun. Alexander named him **BUCEPHALUS**, and the horse carried its master to victory in many battles.

Dog in orbit

In November 1957, the Soviet Union (now Russia) launched a spaceship called *Sputnik 2* carrying a small dog named **LAIKA**. She was not the first animal in space, but she was the **first to orbit the Earth**. She earned a place in history, but *many people protested* because it was not possible to bring her safely back home again.

Fruit flies were the first animals sent into space

Double Dolly

A very special lamb was born in July 1996. Christened Dolly, she was a "**CLONE**" – an identical copy of another sheep. To make her, scientists inserted **the DNA of a cell** taken from one ewe into the egg cell of another. They implanted the developing egg into a *"foster mother" sheep*, who carried and gave birth to Dolly naturally.

Darwin's new ideas

The THEORY that rocked the science world

In 1859, an amateur biologist from England called Charles Darwin published his theory on how all life on Earth evolved from a few common ancestors. The book caused an instant uproar – and changed the course of science forever.

On the *Beagle*

In 1831, Charles Darwin joined a round-the-world *scientific expedition* on a ship called the HMS *Beagle*. Although he suffered from **terrible seasickness**, he still managed to take notes, draw sketches, and collect specimens of many of the plants and animals he came across on his **FIVE-YEAR TRIP**.

The Beagle visited four continents on its epic voyage of scientific discovery.

Nature boy

Charles Darwin came from a **family of scientists**. Erasmus, his grandfather, had written a book called ***Zoonomia***, which suggested that one species of animal could **"TRANSMUTE"** (change) into another. Young Charles became interested in animals and the natural world from an early age.

Erasmus Darwin was also a physician, an inventor, and a poet.

What came after...

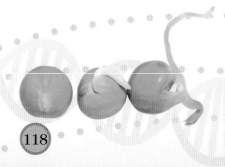

In 1866, Czech friar **GREGOR MENDEL** *published his research on pea plants. He discovered that some traits, such as colour or size, could be passed down from one "parent" plant to the next generation of peas.*

German biologist **AUGUST WEISMANN'S** *work on exactly how animals passed on physical characteristics to the next generation was an important step in the science of genetics.*

Evolving animals

As he travelled, Darwin realized that similar animals showed slight variations in appearance on different islands. Darwin decided that, over many generations, **ANIMALS EVOLVE** (change) to suit their surroundings. Those that *adapt to their surroundings* survive, but those that do not adapt die out – this idea came to be known as the "**survival of the fittest**".

Darwin's book caused an uproar when it was first published.

Controversial claims

Darwin eventually made his ideas public in 1859 in his book *On the Origin of Species*. Some religious leaders were **ANGRY**, as they believed that Darwin's ideas about evolution went against their belief that **God had created all living things**. However, within a decade, his ideas came to be widely accepted.

By the way...

People laughed when I said that humans evolved from apes – we now know that we share 98 per cent of our DNA with chimps.

How it changed the world

Darwin's ideas paved the way for vital breakthroughs in biology, genetics, and medicine.

In 1910, American Thomas Hunt Morgan used **FRUIT FLIES** to show that structures called chromosomes, found in cells, contained all the flies' genetic information.

In 1953, British scientists discovered the **STRUCTURE OF DNA** – the substance that contains the essential code needed for the cells in a living organism to work properly.

Paper plane

The inventors of the first aeroplane were the American brothers **Orville** and **Wilbur Wright**. As children in the 1870s they were inspired by a **PAPER FLYING TOY** their father gave them. It was launched with a rubber band that "pinged" it across the room. The boys thought they'd like to *try flying* themselves.

The Wrights tested out their gliders from 1900 to 1902.

The first flight

The invention of the aeroplane brought distant places CLOSER

Kite-makers

The Wright brothers had little scientific training but they *loved tinkering about* trying to make things work. Their path to fame started with wheels, not wings – they made and repaired bicycles. They also made **kites**, really huge ones, like **GLIDERS**, that could lift a person into the air.

First flight

After teaching themselves some serious aerodynamics and experimenting further with gliders, the Wrights built a **REAL AEROPLANE**. In December 1903 at Kitty Hawk, North Carolina, USA, Orville piloted himself into history, making the **first-ever engine-powered flight**. The plane travelled 36.5 m (120 ft) in 12 seconds. The brothers *made three more successful flights* that same day. Humans had taken to the skies!

Both brothers made two flights each on the day man first took to the skies.

How it changed...

Before aeroplanes, travelling between countries could take weeks or months. Now we can cross the world in hours.

the world

Birdcage brainwave

Very tall buildings were the brainwave of 19th-century American architect **William Le Baron Jenney**. After seeing his wife put a heavy book on top of a *birdcage*, Jenney saw that a **METAL FRAME** could support a great weight. He wondered if it would work for buildings.

The first skyscraper
The high-rise building that changed the look of our cities' SKYLINES

The tragedy of the Chicago Fire cleared the way for the world's first skyscraper.

Did you know?
New York got its first skyscraper in 1889, by which time Chicago already had five.

Great Chicago fire

Jenney **got his chance** to try out his "birdcage" idea in 1871, when large parts of the city of Chicago burned down in a fire and needed to be rebuilt. Within a few years, the architect was *rapidly gaining fame* for his **REVOLUTIONARY** tall building designs.

Jenney studied in Paris alongside Gustave Eiffel, designer of the Eiffel Tower.

How it changed...
Skyscrapers have allowed millions more people to live and work in the world's major cities.

the world

Sky high

Work on Jenney's first **SKYSCRAPER** began in 1884. The ten-storey Home Insurance building was completed in 1885. A lot of people held their breath waiting for the **tower block** to topple over. In fact, it stayed firmly up until 1931, and hit the ground only when *demolished* to make room for an even taller building.

Totally wired

Sending long-distance messages was a slow process before the arrival in 1837 of an electrical communication system called the **TELEGRAPH**. Developed by English inventors William Fothergill Cooke and Charles Wheatstone, it sent **electric messages** via a wire. In the 1870s, the *telephone* did the same for the voice.

With the first telegraph, incoming messages were spelled out on a grid.

Making connections

How superfast global COMMUNICATIONS have changed everything

How it changed...

With telephones, television, and the Internet, information now travels round the world almost as soon as events happen.

the world

Telly addicts

Radio, invented by Italian Guglielmo Marconi in 1895, allowed sound to be **wirelessly broadcast** over long distances. In 1926, the first **TELEVISION** broadcast added pictures to sound. By the 1950s, people took it for granted that entertainment, news, and sports events could be *beamed into their homes*.

By the way...
My World Wide Web whizzes text, sound, and video messages to wherever you want, any time.

Global link-up

In the 1960s, US scientists discovered how to share information by linking millions of computers into a **NETWORK** they called the Internet. In 1990, English scientist **Tim Berners-Lee** (left) invented the World Wide Web, which allows information to be accessed from any computer on the Internet via *websites*.

Soviet satellite

During the Cold War, the USA and the Soviet Union eyeballed one another over the launchpads as they competed to be the **FIRST IN SPACE**. In 1957, the Soviets sent an unmanned satellite, *Sputnik*, into orbit around Earth. They scored again in 1961, when their cosmonaut Yuri Gagarin was the first human space traveller. Spurred on by Soviet triumphs, US President John F. Kennedy vowed that America would put **a man on the Moon** before the end of the 1960s.

Suited and booted for work in zero atmosphere, US astronauts explored the Moon's dusty surface.

Did you know?
The journey to the Moon took us four days and six hours, but we only stayed on the surface for 22 hours.

How it changed...
Space exploration has led to huge advances in our understanding of the Universe and a revolution in communications. **the world**

American Moonmen

On 20 July 1969, with the world watching on TV, American astronauts Neil Armstrong, Edwin ("Buzz") Aldrin, and Michael Collins *touched down* on the Moon's surface in their **SPACECRAFT APOLLO 11**. The USA had achieved President Kennedy's challenge. In all, 12 men walked on the Moon over five more missions before 1972, **but humans haven't been back since**.

Space race

Rival spacecraft blast off in the race to be first on the MOON

And also...

These events cover thousands of years, from the Stone Age to the present day. They are just some of the big moments in BRITISH HISTORY

c.2950–2500 BCE Stonehenge built

When designing a *monument*, Neolithic (New Stone Age) builders **thought big**. One of their finest efforts is a circle of supersized standing stones at **STONEHENGE** in Wiltshire, created as a site for worship and seasonal celebrations.

122 CE Hadrian's Wall goes up

Stretching 117 km (73 miles) across northern England, the 4.6-m (15-ft) high **WALL** was built during the *Roman occupation of Britain*. It sent a stern "keep out" message to **would-be troublemakers** beyond the Scottish borders.

793 First Viking raid

A monastery on the island of **LINDISFARNE**, off northeast England, was the first place in Britain to be **raided by Vikings**. The lightning-quick strike, murder, robbery, and swift exit with the loot would soon become *all too familiar*.

1086 Domesday Book survey

William the Conqueror, king of England, set up a survey to find out *who owned land*, what it was worth, and who owed taxes. The results appeared in the first major public record, the **DOMESDAY BOOK**.

1215 Magna Carta signed

The Magna Carta ("**Great Charter**") was drawn up by the English barons in the reign of **KING JOHN**. It **protected ordinary people** and stopped royalty from doing just what they liked.

1337–1453 Hundred Years' War

England and France really started something when they both tried to **claim the French throne**. The battles and peace treaties went on and on. And on. The French, *inspired by Joan of Arc*, had the **FINAL VICTORY**.

1580 Drake sails around the world

Francis Drake was the first Englishman to *sail around the world*. In 1577, he crossed the Atlantic to South America with five ships and worked his way round to the Pacific, **LOOTING** Spanish ships on the way. He returned home in 1580, down to just one (treasure-loaded) ship.

1591 Shakespeare performed

It is likely that the first of **William Shakespeare's plays** to be performed was the historical drama **HENRY VI PART I**. The actors would have been learning lines for several other plays at the same time, so *they had a lot to remember*.

Shakespeare wrote 37 plays and 154 sonnet poems

1605 Gunpowder Plot

In an attempt to **kill King James I** of England and return the country to Catholicism, *Guy Fawkes* and several fellow assassins stashed barrels of gunpowder under the Houses of Parliament. The plot failed to go with a bang because **FAWKES WAS CAUGHT** before he could light the fuse.

1642–48 English Civil War

To many English people at the time, Charles I was an **UNPOPULAR KING**. War broke out between those who wanted to get rid of him (Roundheads), led by **Oliver Cromwell**, and the royalists (Cavaliers). Cromwell won. *Charles lost his throne, his crown, and his head*.

1666 Great Fire of London

A fire that started in a **bread oven** at a London bakery spread rapidly through the city's tightly packed wooden buildings. When the flames died down four days later, *thousands of homes and churches*, including **ST PAUL'S CATHEDRAL**, were toast. On the plus side, litter, rats, and bugs were also incinerated, giving the filthy streets a good clean.

1825 First steam passenger railway

The locomotive **CHUFFING** along the Stockton to Darlington line in Yorkshire on 27 September was hauling the world's **first-ever steam-powered passenger train**. There was only one proper coach. Most of the hundreds of people who signed up for the two-hour ride were *jolted around in coal trucks*.

1840 Penny post

The postal service was once *very expensive and hugely complicated*. The charges were based on how far a letter had to go and how many pages it had. The unlucky person getting the letter had to pay. Then a man named **ROWLAND HILL** introduced the first-ever flat-rate stamps, **paid for in advance** and costing just one (old) penny. Soon, everyone was madly scribbling letters to everyone else.

1845–49 Irish potato famine

In the mid-19th century, nearly half of all the poor rural families in **IRELAND** ate almost nothing but potatoes. When a plant disease turned the potato crop to *inedible black mush* several years running, a million people died of starvation. **About another million** emigrated in search of a better life.

1880 Compulsory schooling

Until the late 19th century, the law **couldn't force kids to go to school**. Young children often had to work all day in **NOISY FACTORIES** or dangerous mines. To stop this, an Act of Parliament was passed making it law that everyone between the ages of five and ten *had to attend school*.

About 30,000 bombs fell on London during the Blitz

1940 The Blitz

On 7 September 1940, during World War II, German planes appeared over London, **raining down bombs**. This began the "**BLITZ**" (from the German term *Blitzkrieg*, meaning "lightning war"). Raids battered the city for 57 days, while Londoners sheltered from the bombing underground and even slept in tube stations.

1948 Start of the NHS

Before 1948, people *had to pay to see a doctor*. This was tough on those who were poor or out of work. They had to use up their savings (if they had any), try home remedies (which didn't work very well), or just hope to get better. The **NATIONAL HEALTH SERVICE**, introduced by Welsh politician Aneurin Bevan, provided **free healthcare for every British citizen**.

1963 Beatlemania!

The **BEATLES**, a pop group from Liverpool, released their first recording in 1962, but it was not till the following year that Britain went wild over *John, George, Paul, and Ringo*. This was when their song "Please Please Me" hit the airwaves and **changed the sound of pop music** almost overnight.

2015 British monarch beats record

On 9 September 2015, **Queen Elizabeth II** became the longest-reigning British monarch (from 1952) as she clocked up *63 years, 16 hours, and 24 minutes* on the throne. This was when she officially beat the record of the previous titleholder, **QUEEN VICTORIA** (reigned 1837–1901) by one minute.

Glossary

Apartheid
A government programme separating black and white people in South Africa during 1948–1994.

Arab Spring
The series of independent pro-democracy rebellions that took place across the Middle East and North Africa in 2010 and 2011.

Atomic bomb
An explosive nuclear weapon capable of widespread death and devastation.

Capitalism
A system of government where a country's trade and industry are controlled by private individuals and not by the state.

Civil war
A battle between people inhabiting the same country or region.

Cold War
The hostile conflict between the USA and the Soviet Union after World War II, which fell short of actual war.

Communism
A system of government based on workers, where all workers own the country's property, and each person contributes to society according to their ability and needs.

Crusade
A Christian military campaign sanctioned by the Pope.

Emancipation Proclamation
President Abraham Lincoln's order to free slaves across the USA, which was issued on 1 January 1863.

Fascism
An extreme system of government controlled by a dictator, who holds complete power and persecutes those with different views (and often different races or nationalities).

Guillotine
A machine used heavily in the French Revolution from 1789–1799 for execution, consisting of a weighty blade that slices a person's head off when dropped from a height.

Internet
A global system of computer networks allowing millions of people to share words, images, sounds, and videos.

Intifada
This Arabic word for "uprising" that describes the Palestinian rebellions against Israel.

Middle Ages
The period in European history between the fall of the Roman Empire in the 5th century CE and the Renaissance.

Protestantism
A division of the Christian faith, which began as an alternative to the Roman Catholic Church.

Reformation
An attempt at improving the Roman Catholic Church during the 16th century that resulted in Protestantism.

Renaissance
A period of renewed interest in Classical art and culture taking place across Europe from the 14th century onwards. It resulted in some stunning art, architecture, and writing.

Revolution
A rebellion by a group of people aimed at toppling a government to introduce a new system of power, or a massive change in how people live or work.

Senate
A small group of law-makers, most notably the state council of the ancient Roman empire.

Siege
Military action taken to surround and attack a city or fortified structure in an effort to gain control of it.

Silk Road
The ancient trade route between China and the Mediterranean Sea.

Slavery
A system in which one person is the property of another and must obey their orders and work without pay.

Soviet Union
A collection of communist states that was made up of Russia and other parts of the old tsarist empire that came into being after the October Revolution of 1917 and lasted until 1991. Also known as the USSR.

Suffrage
The right to vote in political elections.

Terra Australis
The Latin word for "South Land", this continent was assumed to exist and included on European maps from the 15th century. The name "Australia" was based on this term.

USSR
The Union of Soviet Socialist Republics, including most of the former Russian empire. See also Soviet Union.

Index

Acknowledgements

DK WOULD LIKE TO THANK:
Ann Baggaley and Steven Carton for writing; Carron Brown for the index and proofreading; and Caroline Hunt for proofreading; Priyanka Bansal, Mik Gates, Meenal Goel, Priyansha Tuli, Amit Varma, and Michael Yeowell for design assistance; Bharti Bedi, Rupa Rao, and Sheryl Sadana for editorial assistance; and Nishwan Rasool for picture research.

THE PUBLISHER WOULD LIKE TO THANK THE FOLLOWING FOR THEIR KIND PERMISSION TO REPRODUCE THEIR PHOTOGRAPHS:

Key: a–above; b–below/bottom; c–centre; f–far; l–left; r–right; t–top

3 Corbis: (cb/Head). **Getty Images:** DeAgostini (cb); Hulton Archive (bc). **8 Alamy Images:** Classic Image (cl). **Science Photo Library:** Jose Antonio Peñas (c). **9 Alamy Images:** Gianni Dagli Orti / The Art Archive (br). **Dreamstime.com:** Duccio (clb). **10 Science Photo Library:** Christian Jegou Publiphoto Diffusion (tl); Jose Antonio Peñas (bl, br). **11 Corbis:** Fadil Aziz / Alcibbum Photograph (cla). **Getty Images:** Hulton Archive (bc). **Science Photo Library:** Pascal Goetgheluck (t). **12 Alamy Images:** Everett Collection Historical (crb). **Getty Images:** Universal Images Group (bl). **13 Alamy Images:** Mike Goldwater (tr); Tony Halliday / Art Directors (cl). **Corbis:** Roger Wood (br). **14–15 123RF.com:** moonfish7. **14 123RF.com:** Akhilesh Sharma (bc). **Alamy Images:** M.Flynn (tr). **Fotolia:** Sergey Vasiliev (c). **Getty Images:** De Agostini Picture Library (cl). **15 Getty Images:** Dea Picture Library (tc); CM Dixon / Print Collector (bc). **16 Alamy Images:** Interfoto (tr, bc). **Getty Images:** Universal Images Group / Werner Forman (bl). **17 123RF.com:** Anthony Baggett (bl). **akg-images:** De Agostini Picture Lib. / G. Dagli Orti (tl); Erich Lessing (cra). **Alamy Images:** Peter Barritt (clb). **Corbis:** (bc). **18 Dreamstime.com:** Dmitry Rukhlenko / F9photos (tr). **Getty Images:** Adarsh Kumar / EyeEm (bl). **19 Alamy Images:** Eddie Gerald (tl). **Corbis:** Garry Black / Masterfile (cr). **Dreamstime.com:** Aidar Ayazbayev (bl). **20 Alamy Images:** Ivy Close Images (bc); The teachings of the Chinese philosopher and teacher Confucius (551–479 BCE) became the basis of the moral system known as Confucianism / Ivy Close Images (cra). **Bridgeman Images:** An Ancient Chinese Public Examination, facsimile of original Chinese scroll (coloured engraving), Chinese School / Bibliotheque Nationale, Paris, France (cl). **Getty Images:** De Agostini (bl). **21 Alamy Images:** Ivy Close Images (bl). **Fotolia:** Derya Celik (tr). **Getty Images:** Howard Sochurek / The LIFE Picture Collection (c); Stock Montage (br). **iStockphoto.com:** foto500 (cla). **22 akg-images:** Engraving by Matthäus Merian (1593–1650). (cla). **Alamy Images:** AF Fotografie (tc/Background); Riccardo Sala / age fotostock (tc); The Print Collector (cr). **Bridgeman Images:** (crb). **Getty Images:** A Foot Race at the Olympian Games', Ancient Greece. Artist: Archibald Webb / Ann Ronan Pictures / Print Collector (c); De Agostini (bc). **23 Bridgeman Images:** Pictures from History / Anna Christoforidis and the Capitol Square Review and Advisory Board. (cl). **Dreamstime.com:** Christian Delbert (b); Emmanouil Pavlis (tl). **24–25 Getty Images:** Photo12 / UIG. **24 Dreamstime.com:** Serhii Liakhevych (bc). **Getty Images:** Universal History Archive (bl). **25 Alamy Images:** Niday Picture Library (c/Black Death, bc). **Getty Images:** Danita Delimont / Gallo Images (bl); Hulton Archive (t). **26 Alamy Images:** Photo12 (br); Stefano Politi Markovina (tr). **Corbis:** Don Troiani (clb). **Dorling Kindersley:** Natural History Museum, London (crb). **27 akg-images:** Joseph Martin (tl). **Corbis:** adoc-photos (ca); GraphicaArtis (bl). **Dorling Kindersley:** National Maritime Museum, Greenwich, London (c). **28 Corbis:** Heritage Images (crb); Leemage (c). **Getty Images:** The Print Collector (tr). **Mary Evans Picture Library:** (cla). **29 Alamy Images:** Craig Yates T (c/Train). **Corbis:** (ca); Michael Nicholson (c, cb). **Getty Images:** Edward Gooch (clb); Ann Ronan Pictures / Print Collector (tl). **30 Alamy Images:** GL Archive (crb). **Corbis:** Stefano Bianchetti (t). **Getty Images:** MPI / Hulton Archive (bl). **31 Alamy Images:** Lordprice Collection (cr); The Print Collector (tl); Hilary Morgan (bc); Museum of London / Heritage Image Partnership Ltd (cl). **32–33 Getty Images:** Morton Broffman (c); Charles Shaw (Crowd). **32 Alamy Images:** Archive Pics (bl); India Images / Dinodia Photos (bc). **Getty Images:** AFP (tr); Don Cravens / The LIFE Images Collection (clb). **33 Alamy Images:** Everett Collection Inc (cl). **Getty Images:** H. Armstrong Roberts / ClassicStock (bl); Saul Loeb / AFP (tr); Shel Hershorn / Hulton Archive (bc). **34 Alamy Images:** Gallo Images / Eric Miller (clb). **Corbis:** Hulton-Deutsch Collection (bc). **Fotolia:** skvoor (bl). **Getty Images:** Universal History Archive / UIG (cr). **35 Dreamstime.com:** Sarah Nicholl (ca). **Fotolia:** James Steidl (clb). **Getty Images:** Jean-Pierre Muller / AFP (bl); Trevor Samson / AFP (tl); Pedro Ugarte / AFP (bc). **38–39** Getty Images: DeAgostini (cb). **38 Alamy Images:** Graham Mulrooney (bc). **Corbis:** The Gallery Collection (clb). **Dreamstime.com:** Albo (bl). **Getty Images:** DEA / G. Dagli Orti (tc). **39 123RF.com:** Yang Jun (bl). **akg-images:** Bildarchiv Steffens (tr). **Alamy Images:** Zev Radovan / BibleLandPictures (bc). **Dorling Kindersley:** Archaeological Museum (Arkeoloji Muzesi), Istanbul (c). **Dreamstime.com:** Redbaron (tc). **40–41 akg-images:** (c). **40 Alamy Images:** Vito Arcomano Photography (br). **Dorling Kindersley:** Ermine Street Guard (c, bc). **Fotolia:** Andrejs Pidjass (cb). **41 Alamy Images:** GL Archive (cr). **Corbis:** The Gallery Collection (tr); Image Source (bc). **Dorling Kindersley:** The Trustees of the British Museum (bl). **42–43 Bridgeman Images:** Musee de la Tapisserie, Bayeux, France (c). **42 akg-images:** Erich Lessing (l). **Dorling Kindersley:** The Trustees of the British Museum (bc); National Maritime Museum, London (br). **43 Corbis:** Alun Bull / Arcaid (br); Michael Freeman (bc). **akg-images:** Erich Lessing (r). **44 akg-images:** (tr). **Alamy Images:** Classic Image (cl). **Getty Images:** Photo12 / UIG (cr). **45 akg-images:** IAM Management (bl). **Corbis:** The Gallery Collection (cla). **Dorling Kindersley:** The Trustees of the British Museum (cl). **46 Alamy Images:** Prisma Archivo (crb). **Corbis:** Antonio Capone / SOPA RF / SOPA (bl). **Dreamstime.com:** Svlumagraphica (cr). **Getty Images:** DeAgostini (bc); Stock Montage (c). **47 Corbis:** (br); Tarker (cr). **Dreamstime.com:** Denitsa Glavinova (l). **Getty Images:** Culture Club (bc). **48 Alamy Images:** Gianni Dagli Orti / The Art Archive (c); Kuttig - Travel (clb); Interfoto (tr). **Corbis:** Danny Lehman (bl). **Dorling Kindersley:** Trustees of the National Museums Of Scotland (cb); Pennsylvania Museum of Archaeology and Anthropology (fclb). **Getty Images:** DeAgostini (bc). **49 Alamy Images:** Gianni Dagli Orti / The Art Archive (cl). Corbis: (bl). **Getty Images:** DeAgostini (tr). **Science Photo Library:** NYPL / Science Source (cb). **50 akg-images:** Roland and Sabrina Michaud (tr, crb/Horse). **Dorling Kindersley:** Board of Trustees of the Royal Armouries (crb); Fort Nelson (br, fbr). **Mary Evans Picture Library:** Sueddeutsche Zeitung Photo (bc). **51 123RF.com:** artono9 (bl). **Alamy Images:** Gianni Dagli Orti / The Art Archive (l). **Dreamstime.com:** Lilyforman (bc). **Mary Evans Picture Library:** Interfoto / Sammlung Rauch (c). **52–53 Fotolia:** Mari art (c). **52 Alamy Images:** Classic Image (clb); Niday Picture Library (bc). Corbis: (cra); GraphicaArtis (cr). **Dreamstime.com:** Stanislav Komogorov (tr). **53 Corbis:** Christie's Images (bc); GraphicaArtis (tr). **Getty Images:** Kean Collection / Archive Photos (cb). **54 Alamy Images:** SuperStock (c); World History Archive (cr). **Corbis:** Heritage Images (bc); Historical Picture Archive (cl); Tarker (tr). **Mary Evans Picture Library:** Interfoto / Sammlung Rauch (b). **55 Alamy Images:** IBL Bildbyra / Heritage Image Partnership Ltd (l). **Corbis:** Christie's Images (br); Leemage (tr). **56 Alamy Images:** Fine Art Images / Heritage Image Partnership Ltd (cl); Pictorial Press (bc). **Getty Images:** Prisma (bl). **56–57 Corbis:** Tarker (c). **Dreamstime.com:** Viktoria Makarova (cb). **57 Alamy Images:** Prisma Archivo (bc); World History Archive (bl). **Corbis:** Tarker (tl). **Getty Images:** DeAgostini (tr); Dea / M. Seemuller (cl). **58 Alamy Images:** PA Collection (clb). **Dreamstime.com:** Steve Allen (tl). **Mary Evans Picture Library:** (cr, crb). **59 Bridgeman Images:** Universal History Archive / UIG (cl). **Getty Images:** MPI / Archive Photos (clb); Universal History Archive (cla, c); Hulton Archive (cr); Ann Ronan Pictures / Print Collector (cb). **60–61 Dreamstime.com:** Martina Meyer / Martinam. **60 Corbis:** Leemage (cla). **Mary Evans Picture Library:** Everett Collection (bl). **61 Getty Images:** Art Rickerby / The LIFE Picture Collection (cr); Rühe / ullstein bild (tl). **Mary Evans Picture Library:** Epic (bl). **62 Alamy Images:** Daniel Seidel / Arkivi UG (cl). **Dorling Kindersley:** Fort Nelson (bc). **Getty Images:** Popperfoto (bl). **62–63 Corbis:** Stefano Bianchetti (c). **63 Alamy Images:** Pictorial Press Ltd (bl). **Corbis:** Heinz-Peter Bader / Reuters (cl). **Getty Images:** Art Media / Print Collector (tr); Universal History Archive (bc). **64–65 Getty Images:** American Stock (tc); Popperfoto (c); Bernard Hoffman / The LIFE Picture Collection (cb). **64 Alamy Images:** Schultz Reinhard / Prisma Bildagentur AG (br). **Dreamstime.com:** Denisismagilov (tl). **Getty Images:** Yevgeny Khaldei (clb). **Mary Evans Picture Library:** Photo Researchers (crb); Imperial War Museum / Robert Hunt Library (bc). **65 akg-images:** (bc). **Alamy Images:** world war history (br). **Dreamstime.com:** Denisismagilov (crb). **Getty Images:** SSPL (cra). **66 Getty Images:** Central Press (clb); Ann Ronan Pictures / Print Collector (cl); Keystone-France / Gamma-Keystone (bl); Francis Miller / The LIFE Picture Collection (cr). **Mary Evans Picture Library:** Everett Collection (bc). **67 Alamy Images:** RIA Novosti (c). **Corbis:** (tr). **Mary Evans Picture Library:** Everett Collection (br); Interfoto (bc); Marx Memorial Library (ca). **68–69 123RF.com:** Matthew Antonino (Background); **TopFoto.co.uk:** Lynne Fernandes / The Image Works (c). **68 Corbis:** Patrick Robert / Sygma (bc). **Mary Evans Picture Library:** Tallandier (crb). **69 Corbis:** (bc); Bernd Kammerer / dpa (cr); Peter Turnley (tc). **70 Getty Images:** Esaias Baitel / AFP (crb); Dan Chung / AFP (cl). **71 Corbis:** Sean Adair / Reuters (tl); Sarah Carr / Demotix (cr). **Getty Images:** Spencer Platt (clb). **74 Alamy Images:** GL Archive (c). Corbis: Hoberman Collection (br); Massimo Listri (cla). **Dreamstime.com:** Ron Chapple / Iofoto (tr). **75 Alamy Images:** Lanmas (bc). **Corbis:** Tarker (c). **Getty Images:** Apic (cla); Ann Ronan Pictures / Print Collector (cl). **76 123RF.com:** Mohamed Osama (crb). **Alamy Images:** Interfoto / Personalities (bl); World History Archive (cl). **Corbis:** (bc); Sandro Vannini (cra). **77 Alamy Images:** Erin Babnik (bc); Peter Horree (tl); Classic Image (cra); Interfoto / Personalities (bl). **Dorling Kindersley:** Board of Trustees of the Royal Armouries (clb). **78 123RF.com:** Dmitry Rukhlenko (cra). **Corbis:** Mockford & Bonetti / Eye Ubiquitous (bl). **Getty Images:** Werner Forman / Universal Images Group (bc). **78–79 Dreamstime.com:** Jardach (c). **79 Alamy Images:** Angelo Hornak (tc). **Getty Images:** Werner Forman / Universal Images Group (bl). **80 Alamy Images:** Jim Engelbrecht / Danita Delimont (clb). **Corbis:** adoc-photos (c). **Getty Images:** Keystone-France / Gamma-Keystine (bl); Hulton Archive (bc). **80–81** Getty Images: Apic (c). **81 Alamy Images:** Prisma Archivo (bl). **Getty Images:** Archive Photos (bc); Patrik Stollarz / AFP (cl); DeAgostini (cra). **82 Alamy Images:** North Wind Picture Archives (tl). **Dorling Kindersley:** Museo Archeologico Nazionale di Napoli (bl). **83 Getty Images:** Shone / Gamma / Gamma-Rapho (bl); Popperfoto (tl). Press Association Images: Harry Koundakjian / AP (cr). **84 Alamy Images:** North Wind Picture Archives (cr). **Corbis:** Historical Picture Archive (clb). **Getty Images:** DeAgostini (bc); CM Dixon / Print Collector (bl). **85 Alamy Images:** North Wind Picture Archives (bc). **Bridgeman Images:** Emperor Wu of Han (r. 141–87 BCE) with attendants / Pictures from History (cl); Look and Learn (crb); National Gallery, London, UK (bl). **Corbis:** Paul Starosta (tr). **Dreamstime.com:** Iaroslava Mykhailovska (c). **86 Alamy Images:** Stapleton Historical Collection / Heritage Image Partnership Ltd (tr). **Getty Images:** Fine Art Images / Heritage Images (cr); Universal History Archive (bl). **87 Alamy Images:** Fine Art Images / Heritage Image Partnership Ltd (bl); RIA Novosti (tl, cb); Interfoto / Personalities (cr). **Bridgeman Images:** Tretyakov Gallery, Moscow, Russia (clb). **88–89 akg-images:** (c). **88 akg-images:** Africa Media Online (bc). **Alamy Images:** World History Archive (c). **Corbis:** (bl). **89 akg-images:** (tr). **Bridgeman Images:** National Library of Australia, Canberra, Australia (bl). **Getty Images:** DeAgostini (bc); The Print Collector (cl). **90 Alamy Images:** Chris Hellier (bl). **91 Bridgeman Images:** Peter Newark American Pictures (cr). **Corbis:** Bettmann (bl); Christie's Images (tl). **92 Alamy Images:** North Wind Picture Archives (clb). **Getty Images:** Unidentified Author / Alinari (br); Corbis: The Gallery Collection (ca). **92–93 akg-images:** Pictures From History. **Getty Images:** The Print Collector (c). **93 Getty Images:** DeAgostini (cr); Hulton Archive (c, bc). **94 Alamy Images:** Fine Art Images / Heritage Image Partnership Ltd (cla, clb). **Corbis:** Underwood & Underwood (cr). **Getty Images:** Fine Art Images / Heritage Images (tr). **95 akg-images:** (cr). **Corbis:** (tl). **Getty Images:** ullstein bild (cl); Universal History Archive (bl). **96 Alamy Images:** Dinodia Photos RM (bl); World History Archive (cla). **Corbis:** Bettmann (cra). **Dorling Kindersley:** Board of Trustees of the Royal Armouries (br). **Getty Images:** Margaret Bourke-White / The LIFE Picture Collection (cb). **96–97 akg-images:** Archiv Peter Rühe / GandhiServe (c). **97 Dreamstime.com:** Dmitry Rukhlenko (l). **Getty Images:** Margaret Bourke-White / The LIFE Picture Collection (cra); Keystone-France / Gamma-Keystone (bl). **98 Alamy Images:** World History Archive (c). **Corbis:** David Pollack (bc); Swim Ink (cla, tr). **Getty Images:** Keystone-France / Gamma-Keystone (cr). **99 123RF.com:** Rostislav Glinsky (c). akg-images: Bildarchiv Pisarek (tl). **Getty Images:** Keystone (bl); David Rubinger / The LIFE Images Collection (ca). **102 Alamy Images:** Gianni Dagli Orti / The Art Archive (tl). **Corbis:** Araldo de Luca (ca). **Dorling Kindersley:** The University of Aberdeen (cra). **103 Dorling Kindersley:** Doubleday Swineshead Depot (br). **Getty Images:** Egyptian (tc); Universal History Archive / UIG (cr). **104–105 Bridgeman Images:** Jackson, Peter (1922–2003) / Private Collection / © Look and Learn (c). Science Photo Library: Sheila Terry. **104 Alamy Images:** World History Archive (bc). **Dorling Kindersley:** Natural History Museum, London (bl). **Science Photo Library:** Sheila Terry (crb). **105 Neil Burridge:** (cra). **Getty Images:** Wang Dinghao / ChinaFotoPress (bc). **106 Dreamstime.com:** Rasoul Ali (bl). **Getty Images:** Imagemore Co, Ltd (clb); Time Life Pictures / Mansell (bc). **107 Corbis:** (bc). **Dreamstime.com:** Songquan Deng (bl); Daniel Prudek (tr). **108 Corbis:** Tommy Seiter / imageBROKER (bl). **Getty Images:** Ricardo Liberato (tr). **109 Dreamstime.com:** Piccaya (bl). **110 Corbis:** Zhang Chuanqi / Xinhua Press (tl); (clb, crb). **Getty Images:** DeAgostini (cr). **111 Bridgeman Images:** Pictures from History (cra). **112 Dreamstime.com:** Baloncici (bc). **Getty Images:** DeAgostini (bl). **Science Photo Library:** Sheila Terry (c). **113 Bridgeman Images:** De Agostini Picture Library / G. Dagli Orti (cl). **Dreamstime.com:** Anitasstudio (cr); Bryan Busovicki (bc). **Getty Images:** DeAgostini (bl). **114 Corbis:** (cl). **Getty Images:** DeAgostini (c); Hulton Archive (cb). **115 akg-images:** (tr). **Alamy Images:** The Art Archive (c). **Fotolia:** igor (c/Hand). **116 akg-images:** (bl). **Mary Evans Picture Library:** (cr). **117 Corbis:** Najlah Feanny / CORBIS SABA (bl). **Getty Images:** Sovfoto (cr); Leemage / UIG (tl). **118 123RF.com:** Maria Luisa Lopez Estivill (crb). **Alamy Images:** World History Archive (cb). **Corbis:** (bc). **Dreamstime.com:** Calyx22 (bl). **119 Alamy Images:** The Print Collector (c). **Dreamstime.com:** Captainhe (bl). **Science Photo Library:** Paul D Stewart (cra). **120 akg-images:** (cra). **Corbis:** (clb). **Getty Images:** Science & Society Picture Library (bl). **121 123RF.com:** nito500 (tl/Cage). **Alamy Images:** Pictorial Press Ltd (cra). **Dreamstime.com:** Igor Zakharevich (tl). **Getty Images:** Chicago History Museum (bl, cb). **122 Corbis:** Rick Friedman (clb). **Getty Images:** Time Life Pictures / National Archives (cr); SSPL (tc). **123 Alamy Images:** United Archives / IFTN Cinema Collection (c). **Dreamstime.com:** Gregsi (b)

All other images © Dorling Kindersley
For further information see: www.dkimages.com